the enigma of the mind

HUMAN BEHAVIOR

the enigma of the mind

BY ROBERT CAMPBELL

AND THE EDITORS OF TIME-LIFE BOOKS

TIME-LIFE BOOKS, NEW YORK

The Author: Robert Campbell is a freelance writer, award-winning documentary film maker and composer. As a contributor to Life he wrote major feature stories on scientific subjects including *The Atom, The Human Body* and *The Brain.* He is the author of *The Chasm,* a study of experimental schools in New York City's ghettos, which was nominated for a National Book Award in 1975. He lives with his wife and family in New Jersey.

General Consultants for Human Behavior:
Robert M. Krauss is Professor of Psychology at Columbia University. He has taught at Princeton and Harvard and was Chairman of the Psychology Department at Rutgers. He is the co-author of *Theories in Social Psychology,* edits the *Journal of Experimental Social Psychology* and contributes articles to many journals on aspects of human behavior and social interaction.

Peter I. Rose is Sophia Smith Professor of Sociology and Anthropology, and Director of the American Studies Diploma Program, at Smith College. He is also a member of the graduate faculty of the University of Massachusetts. His books include *They and We, The Subject Is Race, The Study of Society* and *Sociology: Inquiring into Society.* Professor Rose has also taught at Goucher, Wesleyan, Colorado, Clark and Yale, and he has been a Fulbright lecturer in England, Japan and Australia.

James W. Fernandez is Professor of Anthropology at Princeton University. His field research has concentrated on cultural change in East, West and South Africa, and the Iberian peninsula. Articles and monographs on his field studies have been widely published in European and American anthropology journals. He has been president of the Northeastern Anthropological Association and a consultant to the Foreign Service Institute. He taught previously at Dartmouth College.

Special Consultant for The Enigma of the Mind:
Brendan A. Maher, Professor of the Psychology of Personality, and Chairman of the Department of Psychology and Social Relations at Harvard University, is a specialist in abnormal psychology, particularly the disorders of language and thought associated with schizophrenia. A consultant to various governmental agencies, he is also the author of *Principles of Psychopathology* and *Introduction to Research in Abnormal Psychology,* and the editor of *Foundations of Abnormal Psychology, Progress in Experimental Personality Research* and the *Journal of Consulting and Clinical Psychology.*

HUMAN BEHAVIOR
Editorial Staff for *The Enigma of the Mind:*
EDITOR: William K. Goolrick
Text Editor: Virginia Adams
Picture Editor: Adrian Allen
Designer: John Martinez
Associate Designer: Marion Flynn
Staff Writers: Jane Alexander, Carol Clingan,
Richard Cravens, Anne Horan, John Man, Suzanne Seixas
Chief Researchers: Barbara Ensrud, Ann Morrison
Researchers: Oscar C. K. Chiang, Muriel Clarke,
Barbara Fleming, Tonna Gibert, Catherine Ireys,
Gail Nussbaum, Heidi Sanford
Editorial Assistant: Janet Hubbard

Editorial Production
Production Editor: Douglas B. Graham
Assistant Production Editors:
Gennaro C. Esposito, Feliciano Madrid
Quality Director: Robert L. Young
Assistant Quality Director: James J. Cox
Associate: Serafino J. Cambareri
Copy Staff: Eleanore W. Karsten (chief),
Susan B. Galloway, Georgia Ingersoll, Eleanor Van Bellingham,
Florence Keith, Pearl Sverdlin
Picture Department: Dolores A. Littles, Jessy Faubert
Traffic: Carmen McLellan

Valuable assistance was given by the following departments and individuals of Time Inc.: Editorial Production, Norman Airey; Library, Benjamin Lightman; Picture Collection, Doris O'Neil; Photographic Laboratory, George Karas; TIME-LIFE News Service, Murray J. Gart; Correspondents Margot Hapgood and Dorothy Bacon (London), Ann Natanson and Deborah Sgardello (Rome), Maria Vincenza Aloisi and Josephine du Brusle (Paris), Elisabeth Kraemer and Franz Spelman (Bonn), S. Chang and Frank Iwama (Tokyo), Dag Christensen (Oslo), Mary Johnson (Stockholm), Sara Kemezis (Brussels), Mehmet Ali Kislali (Ankara), Robert Kroon (Geneva), Gertraud Lessing (Vienna), Sue Masterson (The Hague), Roy Rutter (Madrid), Jim Shepherd (New Delhi), Bing Wong (Hong Kong).

Contents

Reality Twisted

1

"I didn't want to harm the man. I thought he was a very nice gentleman. Soft-spoken. I thought so right up to the moment I cut his throat." This was a drifter named Perry Smith recalling his role in the brutal slaying of a Kansas wheat farmer, Herbert Clutter, and three members of his family in 1959. The contrast between the mildness of Smith's feelings and the horror of his deed, perpetrated against total strangers, reveals the human mind at its most disordered. At that extreme, the workings of the mind are wholly alien to the average person's experience; he finds them beyond his ability to fathom. But at quite another level, the mind poses mysteries familiar to everyone. Why do some people bite their nails? Or overeat? Or habitually lose things? Or fail to arrive anywhere on time?

Such quirks of behavior are commonplace; others are less so but still widespread. Any random sampling of people is likely to turn up someone who is obsessively neat or compulsively dedicated to work, or the victim of some sort of phobia—a fear of flying, for example, or of driving through a tunnel or being caught in the middle of a crowd. And it is by no means improbable that the same random sampling might reveal one or another individual suffering from formless, unreasoning anxieties, or delusions of persecution, or the effects of a split personality. Whether minor or major, all these are signs of a mind that is not operating the way it should, evidences of behavior that is not entirely "normal"—though defining normality is itself no simple matter.

What stirs up trouble in the mind is a question to which answers are still being sought. In times past, obvious mental disturbances were attributed to the devil or to vengeance wreaked by gods. Newer theories point to inherited defects, an imbalance in body chemistry, or brain circuitry that has gone awry. One of the most widely held 20th Century theories blames unfavorable life experience. In this view, a troubled mind is beset by deep dissatisfaction over such basic concerns as the individual's image of himself; his relationships with other people; and perhaps most important, his inability to gratify fundamental desires and derive pleasure from living. Though an outsider may feel that the individual has no reason to be dissatisfied, what counts is the individual's perception of these matters; it is his mind alone that makes the assessment. As the 17th Century English poet John Milton wrote in *Paradise Lost:* "The mind is its own place, and in it self/ Can make a Heav'n of Hell, a Hell of Heav'n." A modern paraphrase of Milton might go thus: confronted by an intensely frustrating life situation, an individual may correct it, make his peace with it—or succumb to a state of turmoil.

Attempting to unravel the enigma of the mind, behavioral scientists have classified various types of disorders. Among them are neuroses, emotional maladjustments that make life less enjoyable and less rewarding than is warranted by circumstances; psychoses, ailments so disabling that their victims—unlike those afflicted with a neurosis—cannot cope with the ordinary demands of existence; and depression, in which the victim suffers feelings of hopelessness and a loss of self-esteem, and retreats into himself. A depression may be either neurotic or psychotic—or sometimes an expectable reaction to a traumatic event.

Up to this century, mental upsets were accepted as inscrutable facts of life. In severe cases they were treated by priestly incantations, bloodletting, torture or confinement in a madhouse. Today, with research in the behavioral sciences steadily opening up new frontiers of knowledge, approaches to the healing of mental ills are proliferating. They range from "talking therapies"—such as long-term psychoanalysis or short-term counseling—to participation in encounter groups, to the use of certain effective drugs, to so-called behavior modification, a technique by which undesirable behavior is unlearned.

Some innovative therapies employ surprising adjuncts to treatment. Patients are encouraged both to read poetry, in the hope that they may discover that their troubles are not unique, and to write their own verse and thereby perhaps reveal their deep-seated difficulties. Depressed women are invited to watch television soap operas and draw parallels between their own sorrows and those they observe on the screen. Some therapists who deal with disturbed children make a point of keeping pet dogs; they find that their young patients form constructive attachments to an animal. In China, the sayings of Chairman Mao Tse-tung are invoked to try to help psychotic patients distinguish between fact and fantasy.

Of broader significance, there is also a new emphasis on prevention.

An approach known as crisis intervention, which provides psychological first aid in the hope of avoiding serious illness, has become an established field in psychiatry. And researchers are working toward the day when they may be able to spot vulnerable children early and give them special care to ward off future complications.

The need for all these efforts is underscored by statistics. In 1974, one fourth of the 1.5 million hospital beds in the United States were occupied by mental patients, chiefly psychotics. Outside hospitals, therapists were treating another 2.7 million people, most of them neurotics. An estimated 75 per cent of the 26,500 Americans who committed suicide took that way out because of depression. Alcoholism and drug addiction—in some cases symptoms of neurosis, in other cases symptons of psychosis—claimed a heavy toll. About 10 million Americans were alcoholics, at least 65,000 were drug addicts.

In Japan the number of beds in mental hospitals increased sixfold in 15 years. In Great Britain attempts at suicide rose at the rate of 10 per cent a year in the course of a decade, and in one year almost half the entire hospital population were patients with mental disorders. Alcoholism annually accounts for 20,000 deaths in France; it costs West Germany an estimated six million dollars every day.

But statistics tell only a small part of the story. The fact is that most people are susceptible to at least mildly neurotic behavior. Lawrence Kubie, for years before his death one of the world's most influential psychiatrists, maintained that "there is surely in man a universal neurotic potential." Very few individuals fail to display that potential at times, even if it does not develop into a full-blown neurosis. The ways in which it may be shown are seemingly innumerable.

There are, to begin with, what the pioneer prober Sigmund Freud referred to as "the slight functional disturbances in the daily life of healthy people," which he summed up as "the psychopathology of everyday life." A housewife dawdles over her coffee rather than doing chores she subconsciously detests. A clerk makes needless trips to the office water cooler for the same reason. Little "Freudian slips" of the tongue crop up in everyone's conversation.

An example of the Freudian slip that psychiatrists themselves are fond of citing involves a colleague who some years ago was telephoned by a man seeking a consultation. He asked what the fee would be and was told $10—the going rate in those days. He came in for the consultation, and then, when it was over, asked again about the fee, adding: "I don't like to owe money to anyone, especially doctors; I prefer to *play* right away." The use of "play" instead of "pay" made the doctor suspect that the patient was playing with him, and he was right. The man took four dollars from his pocket, then feigned embarrassment; explaining he had no more money with him, he promised to send a check for the rest. After a few weeks the doctor mailed the man a bill for the balance. The letter was returned by the post office marked "addressee not found."

Another common phenomenon is "workaholism," an addiction to work. A graphic description of one such case was provided by the astute wife of a Dutch businessman, who told of a typical two-week holiday with him and their children on the French Riviera. The first day, she wrote, her husband "is worried about what he forgot to do in his business before he left. He makes telephone calls to attend to this. The second day he eats too much and becomes sick at his stomach. The third and fourth he spends in bed. Then he begins to surface. . . . If we can help him survive the first week, he enjoys most of the second week, but toward the end, he becomes preoccupied with all the work facing him when he returns to his office."

Akin to workaholism is what Freud's colleague, the Hungarian psychiatrist Sandor Ferenczi, dubbed the Sunday neurosis. Ferenczi coined the term in 1926, and since then, with the advent of the five-day week, it has become known as the weekend neurosis. Its main symptom is an inability to enjoy free time. The dilemma described by one middle-aged woman is fairly typical. She reported that all week at her job, a very responsible one, she looked forward to weekends. "The thought of having to do nothing is pleasurable," she said, "but when the weekend comes I don't enjoy it. Once it's there, it's boring. I sit and worry. I feel lonely. It's better when I have things to do." In some cases, uneasy feelings during idle hours may represent a fear of facing anxieties that a busy schedule helps to cover up. In other cases, the problem may be a person's nagging conviction that he ought to be doing something besides enjoying himself. Psychoanalyst Alexander Reid Martin labeled as "all too tragically true" the celebrated commentary on 20th Century life in a line of verse by Ogden Nash: "We suffer from hardening of the oughteries."

One everyday psychological disturbance that is rarely recognized as such by those afflicted with it rears up in the form of prejudice. To feel antipathy for a member of another ethnic, religious or national group may be merely a way of going along with the values of an individual's own group—"an unthinking conformity," in the words of Eugene B. Brody, professor of psychiatry at the University of Maryland. But "when the possessor of the attitude avoids confrontation with facts that

His gaze distant and his head sunk, Saul, King of the Israelites, presents classic symptoms of depression in a 16th Century Dutch engraving by Lucas van Leyden. The harp player, looking more like a Dutch plowboy than an Israelite shepherd, is David, attempting to cheer Saul in an early use of musical therapy.

may threaten it," Brody added, "it seems likely that it serves some necessary psychological function for him." One function would be the satisfaction of "a persisting anxiety-based need to demonstrate one's own strength." Whatever inner need it fills, prejudice reflects, as Brody put it, "a functional impairment in reality-testing"—in short, an inability to face facts.

Whether mild or severe, troubles of the mind are to be found among rich as well as poor, in all age groups and in both urban and rural areas. They may affect anyone, anywhere in the world.

Popular belief has long held that psychological difficulties are much more likely to assail city dwellers than countryfolk. The experts consider this a myth. Lawrence Kubie told of a psychiatrist colleague who spent a summer in Canada fishing on a remote lake where "one sturdy family had served for many decades as fishing guides." Before his friend left for home, Kubie recalled, "practically every member of two generations of that family had consulted him about neurotic symptoms that were indistinguishable from those confronting him in his private office and in the outpatient clinic of a New York City hospital."

Freud himself was among the first to question the notion that country living was less hazardous to psychological health. In 1933, nearing the end of a lifetime of pondering human ways, Freud wrote: "In some happy corners of the earth, they say, where nature brings forth abundantly whatever man desires, there flourish races whose lives go gently by, unknowing of aggression or constraint. This I can hardly credit. I would like further details of these happy folk."

A number of investigations have since unearthed "further details" that support Freud's skepticism. The findings do not suggest that city living is easier on the human psyche than people imagine; but they do suggest that country living is harder on it than envious urbanites would like to think.

An investigation, made in 1951 by J. W. Eaton, a sociologist, and R. J. Weil, a psychiatrist, focused on a pacifist sect called the Hutterites. By then this group, of Central European origin, had a history of nearly a century of stable, economically secure life on communal farms in the western United States and Canada. The Hutterites were selected for study because of their reputation for enjoying unusual peace of mind. Entirely self-sufficient, they had never known the pressures of urban living. They were almost completely isolated from the outside world; neither radio nor movies were allowed to intrude. Yet after screening 8,542 men and women, Eaton and Weil estimated that 15 per cent of them were suffering from some mental or emotional impairment. During the same period, a study of a more conventional rural setting, conducted by a Cornell University professor, psychiatrist Alexander H. Leighton, scrutinized 20,000 inhabitants of the Atlantic coast of Canada, most of them living in communities of 100 to 450 residents. The researchers concluded that in what they called Stirling County only 15 per cent of the people could be considered emotionally well. This was essentially the same as the figure subsequently found in another Cornell project, a study of people living in the heart of New York City—the so-called Midtown Manhattan Study.

The study, one of the most intensive investigations of its kind, was begun in 1953 and lasted for eight years. Thomas A. C. Rennie and a team of five social psychiatrists—specialists in the study of mental disorders among population groups—probed the lives of 1,660 men and women between the ages of 20 and 59. The sample was chosen at random from 175,000 residents of a district of Manhattan considered not only typical of New York's white population but also comparable to residential sections of other large American cities. A task force of trained interviewers gathered personal data on each subject for later analysis by Rennie and his colleagues. An interviewer would visit a subject at home for anywhere from two to four hours, recording basic biographical facts and asking a host of questions assembled in a 65-page questionnaire. The questions were designed to try to discover if the subject often was lonely, worried a great deal, thought people were against him, believed things never turned out right for him, and so on.

In the answers compiled by the interviewers, the psychiatrists looked for indications of inadequacy, anxiety and depression; signs of immaturity; tendencies to suspiciousness or to a rigid outlook on life; and evidence that the subject had withdrawn from the world outside. Then they rated the subject's mental health on a scale ranging from zero, "symptom-free" to 6, "seriously incapacitated."

When the psychiatrists tallied the ratings, they found they had placed less than 20 per cent of those interviewed in the zero, or completely healthy, category. All the rest—more than 80 per cent—showed some degree of trouble. The majority, 58 per cent, belonged in categories 1 and 2, with mild to moderate symptoms—such as tension or nervousness —that apparently did not prevent the subjects from getting through the day pretty well. The rest, 23 per cent, fell into categories 3 to 6, which denoted "serious symptoms" in an ascending order of gravity.

One striking discovery made by both the Stirling County and Midtown researchers was that there were far more signs of emotional difficulties, over all, among poor people than among those better off. Of

continued on page 17

Dressed for their parts as railway operators, the Martins stand by a genuine, full-sized signal that embellishes the shed housing much of their model train system. The rest, pecked over by hens, meanders through their country garden.

England's nonconformists

Whenever the 19th Century British philosopher Herbert Spencer traveled by train, he slung himself a hammock to avoid being shaken about. His contemporary, Charles Waterton, who was a naturalist and traveler, shared his bedroom at various times with a sloth, a vampire bat (which he hoped, unavailingly, would bite him) and a 14-foot snake. He once briefly rode a cayman, despite its powerful attempts to throw him off. "Should it be asked how I managed to keep my seat," he said, "I would answer, I hunted some years with Lord Darlington's foxhounds."

This adventurous tradition is still very much alive, for the English are notable among Western peoples for their tolerance—even admiration—of a wide variety of behavior. The original personalities among them are accorded a great deal of leeway in vocations, avocations and habits.

Some Britons debate remote causes at Speakers' Corner in London's Hyde Park. But others pursue unusual life styles, indulge passionate interests in American Indians, spend their days helping animals or construct robots.

Victor and Louise Martin *(above)* adopted the role of railway officials in running 500 model trains through a l930s timetable—with occasional concessions to the present. "During the Suez crisis," Martin said, "we were up all night running troop trains."

Edward and Curly Blackmore (left) live double lives as Sioux (above). They own multitudes of Indian artifacts and clothes, both historic and modern: the dummy at left center is clothed in a contemporary version of Sioux dress. In 1964, Mr. Blackmore, who can converse fluently in sign language, was adopted into the clan of Sitting Bull as "Hunkeshnee" ("Thoughtful"), one of the great chief's boyhood names.

Kate Ward, of Camberley, Surrey, walks a few of the 500 stray dogs she has cared for since she began to devote her life to the job in 1943, after the death of her greyhound Prince. "It's in his name I've done everything," she says.

Decked in a mock space helmet that contains earphones, electronics buff Bruce Lacey nestles close to his robot, named Rosa Bosom, a somewhat forced acronym for Radio Operated Simulated Actress, Battery or Standby Operated Main (i.e., main electrical supply). Rosa, who can move across a room and even deliver a mechanical kiss with her huge lips, was devised to play the Queen of France in a production of The Three Musketeers that ran briefly in London.

Street cleaner "Snowy" Farr works his way through a Cambridgeshire village before his retirement, wearing top hat and tails and pedaling a cart decorated with patterns, horns, dolls and plants.

those in the upper levels in the New York sampling, only one person in eight had difficulties great enough to interfere with everyday functioning, and one in every three was pronounced symptom-free. By contrast, nearly half of the lower-class subjects were impaired, and only one in 20 was rated psychologically sound. Money worries alone did not account for the greater frequency of disturbance among lower-class subjects; other stressful situations that caused trouble were broken families, removal from old neighborhoods by urban renewal programs and the lack of social status itself.

Yet certain difficulties turned up with equal frequency in all classes in the Midtown population. Among these problems were signs of tension and anxiety, including excessive eating, drinking and smoking. Of the severe disorders, schizophrenia—a form of psychosis in which the victim loses contact with his environment and deteriorates emotionally and intellectually—also proved no respecter of class. "Psychotic emperors, presidents, prime ministers and dictators have left their smudged mark on every page of history," observed Dr. Russel Lee of California.

If to be rich or powerful, or both, is no guarantee of perfect mental health, neither is any age immune from psychological trouble. Of particular concern, a rise in the rate and severity of disorders among the young has been detected. The reasons for these changes, according to Illinois psychologist Robert Traisman, are varied: "There is more stress within families, more uncertainty about values to live by, an increase in academic demands on the young, a more automated, less personal society."

Among the results has been an increase in alcoholism in the young. The phenomenon is international in scope. A study in 1974 of students in New York City's schools found that as many as 12 per cent of teenagers were either potential or full-fledged problem drinkers. In the same year, West Germany's Health Ministry estimated that there were at least 60,000 young alcoholics in that country, many only 10 to 12 years old. The extent of the problem among Soviet youth may be gleaned from a report in the Moscow newspaper *Izvestia* that 90 per cent of the inmates in a rehabilitation center for juvenile criminals had been regular drinkers before they were arrested. By 1975, Great Britain had more than a score of Alcoholics Anonymous centers just for youngsters. In France, authorities say that more and more young people are drinking, not out of a normal adolescent urge to prove they are grown-up but to combat a kind of *mal de vivre*, a disaffection with life, that is new among the younger generation. "Habitual alcoholism in French children is a day-to-day fact," according to a French psychiatrist, Suzanne Serin. She cited the case of a three-year-old who often saw "toads and big fishes" in her bed and showed signs of what was erroneously thought to be epilepsy. The child's real trouble was her intake of two large glasses of wine a day. Advised to substitute water, her mother responded with horror: "Tap water! What about microbes?"

No country, no society, no culture is without its share of mental ills. Depression is known the world over. Neuroses and psychoses are found in underdeveloped lands as well as in those that are technologically advanced. In 1966, after studying the members of four African tribes, E. R. Edgerton, an anthropologist, reported they "do not regard a single behavior as psychotic which could not be so regarded in the West."

There are, however, important cultural variations that make perennially fascinating work for behavioral scientists. First, the causes that trigger a mental disturbance can differ from one society to another. Second, although certain basic ailments show up in many cultures, the ways in which they manifest themselves often vary depending on the characteristics of a particular culture. Third, some disabilities are "culture bound"—known in only one society, or at most in a few. Fourth, cultures can differ in the way they size up particular kinds of behavior; actions considered usual in some places are seen as odd in others.

An example of cultural differences in the causes that trigger a mental disturbance was found by American psychiatrist Herbert Hendin in his investigation of suicide in Scandinavia. Denmark and Sweden have remarkably high suicide rates; Norway's rate is remarkably low. Hendin

A glossary of psychiatric terms

Psychiatrists, psychologists and other mental health workers use a special vocabulary in describing and treating illnesses of the mind. Some of the terms were invented by Sigmund Freud, the creator of psychoanalysis and the pioneering explorer of the unconscious mind and its disorders. Others have evolved since his day. At right are terms that are often used—not necessarily in this book, but in conversations and in the specialized literature concerning mental illnesses.

Acrophobia Fear of high places.
Affective psychosis A severe emotional disturbance frequently accompanied by delusions or hallucinations.
Agoraphobia Fear of open places.
Anaclitic depression A depression in an infant caused by separation from his mother, often characterized by weeping, withdrawal illness and a refusal to eat.
Anxiety neurosis Severe apprehension or panic, unconnected to any specific situation, which may be accompanied by sweating and heart palpitations.
Aphonia Loss of voice due to psychological causes.
Autism A form of childhood psychosis occurring most frequently in infants and marked by extreme self-absorption and lack of responsiveness.
Brat syndrome Obnoxious behavior by children involving tantrums and aggressive behavior.
Catharsis The relief of anxiety by releasing suppressed feelings.
Claustrophobia Fear of enclosed spaces.
Clinical psychologist A psychologist specializing in the testing, diagnosis and treatment of emotional disorders.
Conversion hysteria A loss of vision, hearing or other sense despite the lack of physical damage to the sense organ or the brain.
Delusion A persistent false belief.
Depressive neurosis Extreme sadness, dejection and feeling of worthlessness.
Displacement Directing emotions toward a target other than the true one in an effort to avoid conflict—e.g., kicking the wastebasket instead of the boss.
Dissociative hysteria A neurosis characterized by sleepwalking, amnesia or a multiple personality.
Ego The mental manager that weighs desires against conscience and decides what will or will not be done.
Euphoria Exaggerated state of elation.

interviewed nearly 200 Danes, Swedes and Norwegians. Of this number 75 had made serious attempts to kill themselves; the others were relatives, nurses and nonsuicidal patients. To determine what had troubled the would-be suicides so much that they no longer wanted to live, he questioned them intensively about their conflicts, dreams and fantasies, and about the way they had lived and felt from childhood on.

Hendin found that his Danish subjects were often passive and dependent, and that the most frequent precipitant of their suicide attempts was the loss—by separation, divorce or death—of someone they loved and counted on. The Swedes, and the circumstances that disturbed them emotionally, were quite different. "The Swede's ambitiousness and his intensive pursuit of money and material goods seemed as strong as anything seen in the United States, making an American psychiatrist feel at home very soon," Hendin wrote. In his Swedish subjects the most common reason for attempting suicide was self-hatred at failure to reach ambitious goals. By contrast, Hendin concluded, the Norwegians had "less need for suicide as a self-punishment for failure." Many of those he interviewed showed that they would be content to settle for success in fantasy if they could not attain it in reality; when one of the Norwegians did try suicide after a failure to accomplish a goal, it was an expression of anger not at himself but at others.

The symptoms as well as the precipitants of a mental disturbance may vary considerably among cultures. One symptom of schizophrenia, for example, is catatonic stupor, in which a person may adopt and

Hallucination Perceiving something that does not exist.
Hypochondria Imaginary illnesses and excessive worry about health.
Hysteria A name once used for a variety of neuroses.
Id Primitive sexual and aggressive instincts.
Mania Excessive excitement, sometimes accompanied by delusions.
Manic-depressive psychosis A mental disorder characterized by deep swings between elation and depression.
Melancholia A term once used for severe depression.
Multiple personality A form of massive amnesia in which a person forgets who he is and adopts another identity. He may alternate between two, like Dr. Jekyll and Mr. Hyde, or take on many successive identities *(page 25)*.
Neurosis A persistent fear, compulsion or depression that is not justified by

actual circumstances.
Paranoia Delusions of persecution or grandeur.
Phobia Anxiety connected with a particular object, place or situation, such as fear of flying.
Projection An individual's perception of his own anxieties in someone else—even if the other person is free of them.
Psychiatric social worker One trained to assess social adjustments and advise on family and community problems.
Psychiatrist A medical doctor specially trained in treating mental disorders.
Psychoanalysis A therapy devised by Freud in which an individual is guided by an expert to resolve his basic conflicts and anxieties by recalling crucial experiences of his childhood.
Psychosis A severe mental disturbance in which the subject is grossly out of touch with reality.
Psychotherapy A therapy in which an

expert discusses a patient's problems and suggests a course of action. It depends less on deep psychological probing than Freudian psychoanalysis does.
Release therapy A method of treatment in which mentally disturbed children are encouraged to work off their hostility by smashing or breaking things.
Repression The unconscious refusal to think about unpleasant or threatening things.
Schizophrenia A group of psychoses marked by bizarre behavior.
Superego Conscience—the evaluator of the social consequences of courses of action. It serves as an adviser to the decision-making ego.
Transference The psychoanalytic process by which a patient substitutes the analyst for one or both of his parents and reexperiences the childhood feelings evoked by that parent.

Alcoholics Anonymous: the patients who help themselves

Only in recent years has there been a widespread understanding that alcoholism is an illness with deep psychological roots. Ironically, much of the credit for popularizing this view—and for developing perhaps the most effective therapy for alcoholism—must go to a self-styled "recovered alcoholic" named Bill Wilson, who was a cofounder of Alcoholics Anonymous.

A stock analyst with a drinking problem, Bill Wilson took to the bottle in earnest after losing most of his money in the 1929 Wall Street stock market crash. Warned by a doctor that he risked serious damage to his health, Wilson underwent a "transforming experience" and made up his mind to quit drinking. Setting out to convert others,

he discovered to his surprise that discussing his drinking problem with other alcoholics helped strengthen his own resolve to stay off the bottle. He spent a long time talking with an Ohio doctor—and fellow alcoholic—named Robert Smith, and together they founded Alcoholics Anonymous.

Today A.A. numbers among its membership 800,000 recovered alcoholics in 92 countries. Their identities are carefully protected; Wilson and Smith, for example, were known in the organization until their deaths as Bill W. and Dr. Bob. The method members now employ is essentially the same as that of the founders: they help one another by encouragement and by sharing experiences in conquering the drinking habit.

Wilson prepares coffee in the kitchen of his Bedford Hills, New York, home in 1950. He often served coffee at the early meetings of alcoholics held at his house in Brooklyn. The beverage is a favorite of A.A. members, and today a coffee hour traditionally winds up their meetings.

A.A. members at their 1975 international convention in Denver stand with heads bowed in a moment of silence honoring the organization's founders, Wilson and Smith, whose portraits flank the speakers' platform. Marking A.A.'s 40th anniversary, the convention drew 20,000 members from 29 countries.

hold a strained, often bizarre, position for hours at a time. Rather rare in Europe and in the United States, chronic catatonic stupor is frequently found in India and other Asian countries. Some psychiatrists attribute this difference to the fact that Oriental religions advocate withdrawal as a way of responding to difficulties. A catatonic stupor may be an extreme form of withdrawal, but it does not go counter to Oriental cultural beliefs.

In cases of paranoid schizophrenia, a disorder marked by delusions of persecution, an African bushman may identify his tormentors as evil spirits, while a European patient may insist he is the target of X-rays emanating from some malevolent source. One symptom of depression, a profound sense of guilt that is way out of proportion to anything a patient has actually done, is absent in most African and Asian cultures but common in the United States and Europe. The Christian religion puts great stress on conscience and personal responsibility, an emphasis that has its effects on emotional illness as well as on emotional health. African and Asian cultures blame fate and supernatural powers for most of what happens, so that their people, sick or well, have much less to feel guilty about.

A number of aberrations appear only in one culture or just a few. *Koro*, for instance, is reported chiefly among Chinese males. Its main symptom is a terrible fear that the penis is shrinking, that it will disappear into the abdomen, and that as soon as it does, the patient will die; according to ancient superstition, a corpse has no penis, and therefore a man who loses this organ is expected to turn into a corpse. To prevent this dire eventuality, the victim clutches his penis until too tired to hold on any longer. His wife, friends and relatives then take over the task in turn, or a special wooden clasp is applied to hold the penis in place so that it cannot retract into the body.

Another culture-bound mental disorder, *latah*, was first noted in Malaya, but it is also found in Japan, where it is known as *inu*. The symptoms are touched off by fright, caused perhaps by stepping on a snake or hearing of a marauding tiger. The victim, nearly always a person without much status, begins to mimic people around him—usually those who outrank him on the social scale. Then he starts to mumble indistinctly. It soon becomes apparent that he is uttering curses and obscenities. Some Western psychiatrists regard these symptoms as a form of mocking rebellion against authority by an individual who is fed up with kowtowing but would not ordinarily dare to protest.

Perhaps the most intriguing way in which cultures vary is in their views of what constitutes mental illness. The Japanese have always regarded suicide as a proper way out of some difficulties; Westerners consider most suicides an indication of emotional disorder. On the island of Dobu in Melanesia, it is prudent behavior for a housewife to keep a sharp eye on her cooking equipment in order to guard against poisoners, since poison is a frequent local occurrence; in the West, a woman who dared not leave her kitchen unguarded would be marked as paranoid. Not so many years ago, an Eskimo mother often found it natural to accept her son's killer as a replacement for her dead child; most cultures would brand such behavior highly disturbed.

Definitions of mental illness and mental health, of abnormality and normality, differ even among behavioral scientists themselves. Indeed, not everyone believes that mental illness really exists, or that it is recognizably different from mental health.

One of the doubters is R. D. Laing, a Scottish psychoanalyst. Laing asserted that society, not the mental patient, is sick. Psychosis, he argued, is not a disease to be cured but a sane response to an insane world. In Laing's view, the bizarre behavior of a psychotic is mere role playing; he puts on the mask of insanity, a "false self" that serves as a barricade against an ailing society. Behind the mask, Laing believed, the "inner self," or real person, may remain whole and unscarred.

Laing's theories are not popular with most other authorities. Critics have charged that his ideas are unscientific, that he romanticizes the suffering of psychotics as profound social criticism, and that his views rest on mere semantics. They have said that whether or not psychosis is called an illness is irrelevant to the fact that, as one recovered psychotic put it, "schizophrenia is sheer hell for millions of people." And Laing's own case studies of psychotics imply that schizophrenia really is a mental affliction—despite the author's avowed philosophical stance.

Another dissenter from the idea that mental normality and abnormality are definable realities is the American psychoanalyst Thomas Szasz. To Szasz, "the concepts of mental health and mental illness are mythological concepts," malign inventions that permit society to ostracize people it does not like; he described psychiatrists as "manufacturers of madness" whose self-esteem is bolstered by labeling some people mentally ill and then looking down on them as inferior. Szasz's objection to the term mental illness is based partly on the idea that "the mind is not an organ or part of the body" and "cannot be diseased in the same sense as the body can." The so-called mentally ill, he said, have "nothing wrong with their bodies."

This argument is becoming increasingly uncertain as scientists turn up evidence suggesting that certain mental afflictions do have biological underpinnings *(Chapter 5)*, although they may need an environmental stimulus to trigger them. Szasz's view, like Laing's, seems to be largely semantic. He acknowledged that many of the people other psychiatrists call mentally ill are unhappy and want help, and he himself treated patients—although, he said, "I don't call it therapy; I call it plain talk." Sometimes he even seemed to be conceding that emotional disturbance is a reality and that no one escapes it. "Everybody has problems about how to live," Szasz insisted. "If you want to know who's mentally ill, look in the mirror while you're shaving."

A third dissenter from conventional psychiatric ideas about normality and abnormality is D. L. Rosenhan, a California psychologist. Rosenhan conducted an experiment in which eight researchers—three psychologists, a pediatrician, a psychiatrist, a painter, a housewife and a student—pretended to be insane and were admitted to 12 different hospitals in all, in five states on the East and West coasts of the United States. The results were entertaining—and illuminating.

All the pseudo patients complained they heard voices saying the words "empty," "hollow" and "thud." All eight were diagnosed as psychotics. Admitted to psychiatric wards, all eight then resumed their usual behavior and spent much of their time taking notes on what was going on around them. In one instance, ward attendants apparently interpreted the note-taking as a sign of abnormality. "Engages in writing behavior," ran the daily nursing report on the researcher. Not one of the pseudo patients was detected—except by some of the real patients. Many of these asserted, "You're not crazy. You're a journalist, or a professor. You're checking up on the hospital." Eventually (it took from seven to 52 days) the researchers persuaded hospital staffers that they had recovered enough to be released. Rosenhan's conclusion: "We now know that we cannot distinguish insanity from sanity."

In fact, while the experiment does reveal much about mental hospitals, including the frequent lack of individual attention for patients, the conclusion has been refuted by, among others, psychiatrist Seymour Kety, one of the world's leading researchers in mental illness. Kety made his point by hypothesizing a similar attempt to mislead physicians with faked symptoms of a physical ailment, such as a severe ulcer attack, which can make a patient vomit blood. Suppose, he said, that he drank a quart of blood, concealed what he had done, and then appeared in the emergency room of a hospital vomiting blood. The doctors there might well conclude that he had a bleeding peptic ulcer. That he had misled them by faking his symptoms, Kety noted, does not prove they do

The twenty-one faces of Eve

Chris Sizemore displays the painting entitled *Three Faces in One*, which she executed to symbolize her multiple personalities. At 48, after 18 years of psychoanalysis, Mrs. Sizemore succeeded in achieving one integrated personality.

Behind the pensive gaze of Chris Sizemore *(below)* lies a bizarre secret. She is the real-life heroine of *The Three Faces of Eve,* the famous film about a case of multiple personality, a woman who in effect was not one person, but three people with dissimilar characteristics.

The story began for Chris at the age of five, when her grandmother died and her mother made her kiss the corpse. A psychiatrist later concluded that the experience had triggered a psychological breakup in the girl. After that Chris was different people in turn. One of them, whom her psychiatrist called Eve White, was demure, retiring, almost saintly. Another—Eve Black—was a vain, rowdy, irresponsible woman who once tried to strangle her child. A third was Jane, a subtle mix of Eve White and Eve Black. The film was made about these three personalities. Chris was then 25 years old.

By her doctor's count, she later went on to assume 18 other personalities. One was the Spoon Lady, who collected spoons, another was the Blue Lady, who wore only that color. Some could sew or drive a car; others lacked those skills. At last, in 1975, Chris was declared fully recovered, and she revealed that she was the subject of the movie.

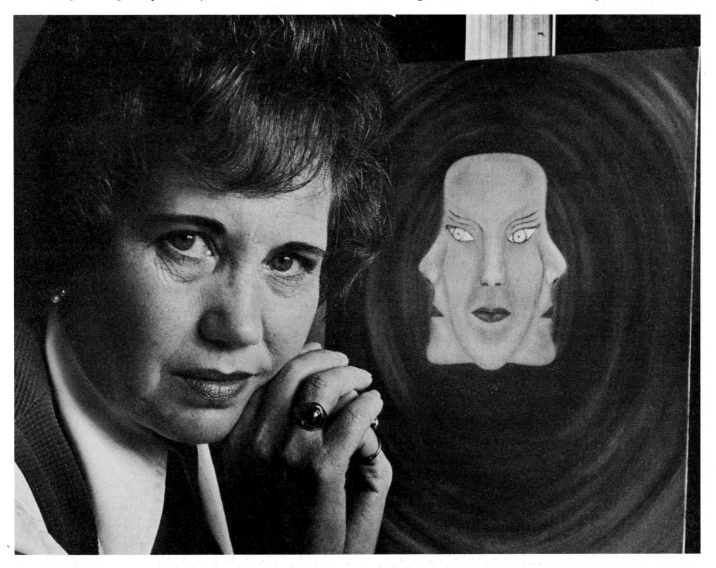

not know how to diagnose genuine cases of bleeding peptic ulcers.

Most experts take issue with the extreme opinions of Laing, Szasz and Rosenhan. Nearly all agree that abnormality exists and is easily detected in the grossly distorted behavior of the psychotic. Many are much less certain about how to spot—and to define—behavior near the other end of the broad spectrum of mental troubles. For then it becomes necessary to agree on what is "normal" human behavior. There is no single way to define normality that cannot be challenged on one ground or another. Some authorities believe that normality is definable, but each is likely to have his own pet ideas on the subject and to find it difficult to agree with his colleagues on any one description. Normality is not an objective but an evaluative concept, a matter not of absolute fact but of subjective opinion.

Of the many definitions of normality that have been proposed, most fall into one of three categories. The first is based on social deviance, on a comparison of an individual's discernible behavior with the behavior of others. The second relies on scientific reality, comparing an individual's perception of measurable things with coldly objective measures of those things. The third definition of normality depends on the individual's own assessment of his "happiness." Of these definitions, the most troublesome, in some respects, may be social deviance.

Some social-deviance definitions equate normality with average behavior; a person is normal if he is statistically similar to the majority of human beings. By that test, neuroticism is normal, because most people show some signs of it. Among the critics of this definition, Lawrence Kubie, arguing by analogy, noted that "dental caries is not 'normal' merely because most of us have cavities in our teeth."

By other social-deviance definitions, normality means conformity to widely held beliefs or to conventional ways of behaving. History is full of examples of the pitfalls of this view. For hundreds of years, failure to embrace Catholicism was defined by the Church as abnormal. Since magic and occultism were forbidden, their practitioners were considered heretics and were thought to be mad, or bewitched or possessed by Lucifer and his demons, and they were looked upon as dangerous.

In 1231, Pope Gregory IX moved to combat the abnormality of heresy and the threat it posed by establishing a tribunal, known as the Inquisition, to track down and punish heretics. Massive witch hunts soon got underway. To identify witches, inquisitors looked for *stigmata diaboli*, signs of the devil which were bodily defects or malfunctions supposedly inflicted by Lucifer to mark his human collaborators. If necessary, a confession of heresy was extracted by torture. Then the demons responsible for the victim's lack of faith were cast out in rites during which onlookers firmly believed that they saw little devils streaming from the mouth of the possessed. The witch—usually a woman—was often required to repeat her confession in open court. Her head and genitals were shaved so that no devil could hide there, and she would be brought into court backward to prevent her from casting an evil eye on the judge. Then she would be stripped of her clothing to reveal her stigmata, and when her confession had been heard, she might be burned at the stake "to free her soul" and to "purify" it by fire.

The popular view of psychiatrists —especially the notion that they assume they can get answers of deep significance by asking simple questions—is gently spoofed in the comic strip Peanuts at right. The episode is a favorite of the strip's creator, Charles Schulz. But he denies that he uses Lucy van Pelt —who is perhaps the world's most famous unlicensed psychiatrist—to ridicule psychiatry; rather, he says, he intends Lucy, dispensing her waspish advice to Charlie Brown from a street booth, to mirror the world of his experience.

A more recent example of nonconformity defined as abnormality is the case of Zhores Medvedev, a Soviet biochemist who incurred his government's displeasure by publicly questioning the objectivity of science under Stalin and by advocating that scientists around the world be allowed to meet freely to coordinate their research. In 1970, three police officers and two psychiatrists burst into Medvedev's apartment and carted him off to a mental hospital. Committees of psychiatrists interviewed him at length and tried to prove from his answers that his ideas about science stemmed from psychological derangement. They pronounced him a "psychopathological personality" and maintained that he suffered from "poor adaptation to the social environment" and from "paranoid delusions of reforming society."

The psychiatrists could not make their diagnosis stick because, even in the Soviet Union, it was seen to be an obvious abuse of the social-deviance definition of normality. Medvedev's brother Roy, a noted historian, attested to Zhores' normality and protested his confinement vociferously. So did eminent scientists and artists around the world. After 19 days, the medical bureaucracy let Medvedev go home.

From such cases as these, it is obvious that defining normality in terms of social deviance has many flaws. Values change, and what is normal in one time or place becomes abnormal in another. Equating deviance with abnormality opens the way to political oppression, and at least theoretically it is possible for the unscrupulous to banish not only political foes but also, for personal reasons, people who just happen to get in their way. In 1728 the English journalist and novelist Daniel Defoe, author of *Robinson Crusoe*, issued a public polemic against "the vile Practice now so much in vogue among the better Sort, as they are called, but the worse sort in fact, namely, the sending their Wives to Mad-Houses at every Whim or Dislike, that they may be more secure and undisturb'd in their Debaucheries."

Nowadays, legal safeguards make that kind of abuse very rare. But it is also true that among people who are genuinely disturbed many are committed to mental institutions against their will. Thomas Szasz maintained that even this practice is unjust: "I am unqualifiedly opposed to involuntary mental hospitalization and treatment. To me, it's like slavery: the problem is not how to improve it, but how to abolish it," he added. "We have managed to repackage the Inquisition and are selling it as a new, scientific cure-all."

When Szasz first came to this conclusion in the 1950s, it was a minority view. By 1975, many thoughtful men and women were beginning to agree with him, at least in part. In that year the U.S. Supreme Court

Unusual departures from standard behavior may be winked at—in some circumstances, at some times. When the Traffic Director, as police affectionately call this unofficial assistant, waves cars through one of New York's busiest intersections, he does it so expertly he is allowed to take over briefly, and motorists unquestioningly obey his commands.

ruled that emotionally sick Americans could not be confined against their will and without treatment if they were dangerous to no one and capable of surviving on the outside. Justice Potter Stewart wrote for the majority on the court: "May the state fence in the harmless mentally ill solely to save its citizens from exposure to those whose ways are different? One might as well ask if the state, to avoid public unease, could incarcerate all who are physically unattractive or socially eccentric."

Increasingly, then, social deviance is coming under fire as a basis for defining normality. Definitions grounded in scientific reality are somewhat less vulnerable to criticism. By this kind of standard, behavior is abnormal if it does not reflect things as they actually are: not as somebody imagines them to be but as objective measures establish them. In this sense it is abnormal for a person to believe that his legs have turned to glass, or to hear voices in rooms that are demonstrably empty and beyond the reach of voices from outside.

One trouble with this measurable-reality definition of normality is that it often takes time to discover objective truth. Many instances of apparent paranoia turn out to be valid when all the facts are finally in; some people who think they are victims of persecution are actually being persecuted. In many more cases, no amount of time will resolve the doubts; the facts can never be learned.

The third type of definition equates normality with happiness, or with something akin to happiness—the absence of "undue" or "excessive" anxiety, nervousness or tension. This was the measure of normality used in the Midtown Manhattan Study. Some critics object that it is impossible to be precise about the meaning of undue or excessive. Others ask whether it is normal or realistic to be completely happy and anxiety-free in a world menaced by pollution, corruption and the H-bomb; psychoanalyst Rollo May described it as normal and in fact desirable to suffer from "existential anxiety," which he defined as "the anxiety of a man facing the limits of his existence with its fullest implications: death, nothingness."

Still other critics suggest that happiness may, in fact, be a sign of abnormality. They cite a study by psychiatrists at the University of Minnesota. The investigators chose as their subjects 50 men, all 26 years old, who had been tested in school 12 years earlier, when 83 per cent were pronounced normal. In the interim few had shown any signs of emotional disturbance. Retested, the subjects were rated as very normal. Most loved their wives and children, enjoyed sex, liked their work and did it pretty well, and felt generally contented.

The doctors in the study admitted that their subjects seemed rather dull and unimaginative. Some outside psychiatrists went further. One critic observed: "Two of the significant findings about these normal men were their extraordinary degree of contentment and freedom from anxiety. I don't necessarily equate these qualities with normality. Almost every person is continually interacting with his environment and the people in it. Since there are bound to be many conflicting aims among the people with whom he associates, it would be expecting the impossible for a healthy person to be in a continual state of contentment or placidity. I would say that these men were *ab*normal."

Additional objections have been raised to the normality-as-happiness definition. Suppose a person feels contented and generally functions well, without experiencing anxiety. The absence of symptoms could be taken to mean that he is normal, yet he may have hidden difficulties that will someday prove his undoing. By analogy, a person with an undetected cancer is not in normal health and may die of his disease. The same outcome is also possible for a man who shows apparently minor mental symptoms. A successful lawyer had a seemingly harmless compulsion to button and unbutton his vest. He was not unhappy about his symptom; in fact, he seldom thought of it and most observers would have judged him essentially normal. But one day his preoccupation with his vest buttons kept him from paying attention to the traffic, and he was almost killed crossing the street. His compulsion was therefore not insignificant because it had the potential for killing him.

Given all of the flaws in the foregoing definitions, it becomes clear they have failed to establish a universally accepted standard of what constitutes untroubled versus troubled behavior. That may, indeed, remain an elusive goal; among other reasons, the various cultures that make up the tapestry of mankind differ too widely.

Yet there is a common theme in these definitions, one that applies in all societies. Whatever the cause of an individual's troubled behavior —a conflict within the unconscious, a biochemical imbalance, or both —the effect is to handicap him in some way. He may be unable to perceive or react to his environment as other people do. Or he may be aware of his environment, yet act in a manner unacceptable to his society —a handicap whether he agrees with society's judgment or not. Or he may have habits he would like to change but cannot.

Defining behavior in terms of whether or not it hinders the individual in dealing with himself and his world has one surpassing virtue: it takes a highly practical view of the matter. The same spirit of pragmatism now infuses other efforts to penetrate the enigma of the mind. After centuries of intuitive theorizing, behavioral scientists are more and more concentrating on finding facts. Some basic causes of mental problems today stand revealed. And even when causes remain obscure, solutions to the problems are taking the form of down-to-earth treatments —some so effective as to seem miraculous.

Strategy for a widow's trauma

Even the healthiest of persons, moving through life smoothly and happily in a familiar routine, can have the props knocked out from under him so suddenly and severely that he will develop serious neurotic symptoms. The crucial blow may be the loss of a loved one, a career setback or a catastrophic financial reverse. Whatever the cause may be, the effect can be paralyzing, sapping the strength and undermining the will so effectively that the victim often is unable to go on without some kind of professional help.

For Frances Markowitz, the 58-year-old New Jersey woman at right, the critical event was the death of her husband. During her 31 years of marriage she had centered her life upon him and their two daughters. In the process, she became totally dependent on her family. When her husband, Jack, died unexpectedly in 1971, she was gripped by a paralyzing depression. Mrs. Markowitz could not continue to work, became painfully dependent on her daughters, and reached a point where she felt helpless and adrift.

Yet despite all her mental turmoil she retained the will to survive. She sought help, and on the advice of a psychiatrist joined a highly structured program of self-help designed for "normal people with problems," called the Strategy for Living Program. Through the program, she was forced to look at her life candidly and make herself start functioning again. So effective were the results of her efforts that she offered to share her experience with photographer Charles Harbutt, in the hope that it might be helpful to other people who have similar problems.

On the wall beside Frances Markowitz are highlights of her happy, but haunting, past. Jack Markowitz, shown with his daughters, is in the photograph at left center. Recalling his death, she says: "I went blank. I was totally happy with my family, my husband. I didn't have any outside interests. I wasn't prepared."

PHOTOGRAPHED BY CHARLES HARBUTT

Guidance from other sufferers

When Fran Markowitz took her troubles to psychiatrist Ari Kiev *(below)*, he offered no miracle cure. He told her essentially what a compassionate uncle would have: accept the sadness of death as normal, trust yourself and get moving. But Kiev was able to help in a way the wisest uncle could not, for he had a mechanism to get her to follow his advice: group counseling in the Strategy for Living Program.

She and other women who were enrolled in the program met weekly with group therapist Lynn Okerson *(near right)* to discuss their problems and provide one another support in surmounting them. The group prompted Mrs. Markowitz to plan a step-by-step campaign for independence (first item: driving a car). Every week she had to report progress. If she faltered, the group prodded until she acted.

Consulting with psychiatrist Ari Kiev (foreground), Mrs. Markowitz learned that her virtual paralysis in daily affairs was a common reaction to the death of a husband. Dr. Kiev suggested group counseling as a way of ending the depression and of helping her to establish a fresh pattern of activities.

In a meeting with her Strategy for Living group, Fran hears a fellow member describe problems encountered in finding a job. In such sessions, the exchange of experiences helps each member attack her difficulties with renewed confidence.

Still not entirely relaxed behind the wheel, Mrs. Markowitz practices to gain confidence.

Learning to manage alone

One thing that Fran Markowitz had to be able to do if she was to resume a normally active life was seemingly simple: drive a car. Automobile transportation was essential in the huge, sprawling suburb where she lived. She knew how to drive, but her husband had done most of the driving during their married life, and she panicked at the thought of taking the wheel herself.

Now the support of the Strategy for Living group proved its value. Mrs. Markowitz' fellow members insisted on her using her car and she hesitantly obeyed. "I got into the car and drove it around the block. The next day, I did the same thing—only a little further. Soon I was getting about with no trouble and even beginning to enjoy it."

Mrs. Markowitz argues with a garageman after learning that her car—in the shop for a paint job—will not be ready on schedule. Previously, the automobile's upkeep had been handled by her husband. Slowly, she assumed responsibility for the car as part of her efforts to strengthen her control over her life.

Mrs. Markowitz' employer asks her comments on a proposed new color scheme in the apartment complex that she manages. Her duties included handling all rentals, supervising a staff and dealing with the complaints of tenants.

Lunching alone in a restaurant gives Mrs. Markowitz a chance to relax. She used such breaks to schedule her afternoon work. But these moments also proved to be reminders of the loneliness that remained an inescapable part of her life.

Making a career of a job

Although Fran Markowitz had worked throughout most of her marriage—and held a responsible position as manager of a 240-unit apartment complex—she had never viewed outside employment as an integral part of her life. This attitude, coupled with her depression after her husband's death, made it so hard for her to cope with her job that she stopped going to the office altogether.

But fortunately, Mrs. Markowitz' employer was sympathetic. And the Strategy for Living group helped her to see her job in a different light, as a demanding but rewarding way of serving others. She returned to the office—at first for a few hours a day, then gradually increasing her work load until she put in a full day. Soon she found that her career accomplishments contributed to her growing sense of self-esteem.

In the bustle of her office, Fran Markowitz tries to interview a prospective tenant.

Mrs. Markowitz (second from left) stretches in a side-bending exercise in the calisthenics class she joined. Although she was not previously interested in athletics, she found the exhausting 45-minute workout "makes me feel great."

The challenge of new interests

Buoyed by a newfound mastery over her daily routine and prodded by the Strategy for Living group, Fran Markowitz looked for experiences to enrich and broaden her life. "They were constantly telling me to try something new, something different," she said.

She was soon embarking on excursions to museums, shops and theaters. And her fascination with the psychological changes that she had experienced stimulated her curiosity about programs for personal improvement. She joined a calisthenics class that kept her figure trim. She became an avid reader. And she also took up transcendental meditation, or TM. "I have a practical mind," Mrs. Markowitz said, "and TM seemed a logical way to relax the nervous system completely."

Twice daily, Fran Markowitz relaxes by using transcendental meditation techniques.

Pursuing her curiosity about her attitudes and behavior, Mrs. Markowitz scans bookracks for works dealing with psychology. She became especially interested in writings about self-help and the techniques of mental discipline.

A close family— at arm's length

One reason Fran Markowitz worked so hard to restore a normal balance to her life was her relationship with her daughters. She had become dependent on them during her mourning, and neither she nor they could accept her lack of self-reliance. "It tore me apart, knowing that they felt guilty, anxious— wondering if I was all right," she recalled. Eventually her renewed activities gave her a life of her own and, at the same time, a relaxed, open rapport with her family. She began to visit her grandchildren, to go shopping with her daughters and to hold social gatherings at her new apartment.

Her experience led Mrs. Markowitz to caution her daughters "to be as independent as they possibly can, and to have a busy life outside of their family and children. It was painful for me to say that to them. But I was never prepared for the death of my husband. If I had been, I would have had more interests, more goals of my own. It would have helped."

During a visit, Mrs. Markowitz laughs as her grandson tries to kiss through the glass door.

On a shopping excursion with one of her daughters, Mrs. Markowitz inspects a bracelet that she has purchased. With her new self-reliance, she found that she enjoyed her children but was not dependent on them for emotional support.

Mrs. Markowitz now entertains friends and family on special occasions, such as the celebration below. The 11 guests in the dining room erupted in laughter at their hostess' choice of food for a Jewish New Year feast—meatballs and spaghetti.

Late in the evening, Fran Markowitz sits in her den and listens to one of the tapes that Dr. Kiev has prepared for the members of his Strategy for Living Program. The tapes offer advice for coping with the fears, loneliness and challenges that she might encounter. "I still don't have all the answers," she confessed. "But I feel confident about the future. The secret—my entire philosophy now—is to think, 'I can.'"

Neurosis: Universal Ill

For reasons Freud himself might have enjoyed exploring, the terms he and his colleagues applied to the intricacies of human behavior have become staples of everyday speech. Never has the jargon of specialists been more warmly embraced by the general public. Such words as neurotic, inhibit, repress, sublimate, introvert, extrovert, compulsion and obsession turn up in casual talk at parties and clubs, in universities and markets. None of these terms was in common use before this century, and their currency today attests to their importance. All refer to some aspect of neurosis, the most common of psychic ailments. The words are not mumbo jumbo, for they identify and help explain troubling behavior that in times past could not even be recognized for what it was. They enable everyone to see inside himself—and others—to understand, with a clarity never before possible, why people act as they do.

The nature of a neurosis is summed up in Freud's own description of its victim as someone who is "at war with himself." In extreme cases the war may take the form of a running battle that seriously incapacitates the sufferer and so torments him that he longs for death. More often it takes the form of skirmishing in which the damage is limited enough to permit the victim to manage other aspects of his life without much difficulty. Unlike the much more seriously ill psychotic, the neurotic keeps a relatively clear view of reality; his personality is not disorganized; he has no delusions or hallucinations, no "crazy" ideas. Usually he is aware that all is not well with his psyche.

Almost everyone sees the signs of neurosis in people around him and recognizes the minor symptoms that, at one time or another, inevitably develop in himself. They may be nothing more than finickiness—the housewife who empties ash trays before her guests have finished using them—or an inability to keep appointments on time. There is the man who is so afraid of flying he gives up travel that he would enjoy, the child who always seems to suffer from a cold on school days but is miraculously cured on vacations and weekends, the mother who cannot shake off fears for her children's safety, the worker who frequently suspects fellow employees of plotting to get him discharged.

Neurotic responses take countless forms, many of them bizarre, but all share one chief characteristic: anxiety. The dictionary defines the term as an uneasiness or dread stemming from the fear of a real danger or misfortune, but psychologists make a crucial distinction. They use the word to describe a dread or painful foreboding not accounted for by external circumstances. It feels like fear but is unjustified. An example of the difference was cited by the psychoanalyst Karen Horney: if a person is afraid whenever he stands on a high place his reaction is called anxiety, but if he is afraid on a particular occasion when he loses his way on a mountain in a storm, his reaction is called fear. In other words, Horney wrote, "Fear is a reaction that is proportionate to the danger one has to face, whereas anxiety is a disproportionate reaction to danger, or even a reaction to imaginary danger." It is the disproportion of the reaction to reality—everyone, after all, must empty ash trays sometime—that signifies neurosis.

Sometimes anxiety is chronic, causing such symptoms as nervousness, tension, dizziness, inability to concentrate, butterflies in the stomach, indigestion, insomnia, impotence or frigidity. Sometimes the anxiety is acute. It may strike like a heart attack and it is often mistaken for one. The victim's face pales, he sweats, his pulse races and sometimes he gasps for breath so agonizingly that he is rushed to a hospital—where examination shows his heart to be normal.

Anxiety is the predominant characteristic of one of the most common neuroses—called simply anxiety neurosis, since the anxiety seems unconnected to any one situation—but it is also a feature of three other important types of neuroses, categorized as phobic, obsessive-compulsive and conversion. Each of these, however, has more specific traits as well.

In people with a phobic neurosis, anxiety is connected with a particular object, place or situation. A junior executive would like to move up the corporate ladder but fears success and finds excuses to turn down promotions. The boy who wakes up seemingly ill every weekday morning dreads school, and if his mother lets him stay home, the illness vanishes. Unreasoning terror of success or of school are but two of a virtually endless list of phobias, including such specialized forms as acrophobia, unjustified fear of heights; agoraphobia, of open spaces; claustrophobia, of closed spaces; ailurophobia, of cats; ergophobia, of work; brontophobia, of thunder; and pyrophobia, of fire.

Victims of obsessive-compulsive neurosis suffer from a different type of problem. They are plagued by unwelcome thoughts or an urge to do things that are irrational and often self-destructive. Obsessive thoughts may rivet on single words, frequently obscene or profane, or on tortuous ideas—for example, fantasies of injuring a close relative or friend. Compulsive acts range from harmless mannerisms, such as repeatedly twisting a lock of hair, to troublesome rituals, such as constant hand washing, to self-defeating patterns of living.

The compulsive neurotic may not recognize the driven quality of his behavior. A woman who made a successful career as a lawyer regarded herself as unlucky in life because at the age of 35 she was still single; yet she kept prospective husbands away by dating only married men. She may have thought she was simply unfortunate in being drawn to such men; she did not realize she was *choosing* them. Some sufferers do know their behavior is unrewarding and yearn to correct it, but any attempt to do so brings terrible anxiety. As one compulsive hand washer described it: "I'm so afraid of germs, I wash my hands till they are red and sore. I just feel chained and I don't know how to get out."

The other main type of neurosis, conversion, has become increasingly rare in recent decades—perhaps because it seems to strike someone who tries to hide psychological conflict, and people today are less inhibited about discussing their woes. This ailment gets its name from the fact that an emotional problem is converted into a physical symptom—even though nothing is wrong with the victim's body. In one case the daughter of divorced parents began to have daily attacks of vomiting; the trouble was not her digestive system but her father's remarriage. Other conversion hysterics develop temporary paralysis, blindness, deafness or other disabilities. The victims often show remarkable unconcern about even the most serious physical symptoms. Puzzling as their indifference may seem to their families, there is an explanation. The sufferer may reap benefits from a hysterical ailment—either by winning sympathy or by shifting the worry to others.

There are two schools of opinion as to what in the mind causes neurosis, and they lead to two quite different methods of treatment. The newer "social learning" school holds that neurotic behavior is made up of self-defeating habits an individual acquires from experiences; they are learned as any habit is learned and can be unlearned. The older, "psychodynamic," school, taking its cue from Freud and later psychoanalysts, holds that neuroses are not learned habits but the indirect (seemingly irrelevant) expressions of unconscious conflicts, usually arising in childhood, between contending forces in the mind. In this view the struggle ordinarily is between the person's conscience and his wishes, especially sexual and aggressive urges, and it is this struggle that must be addressed, not the behavior that signals its presence.

To understand the psychodynamic explanation of neurosis requires at least a little knowledge of Freud's ideas on how the psychic apparatus develops and how it works. The mind, he believed, is divided into three parts—id, ego and superego. At birth, the mind consists solely of the id—primitive, driving instincts. Some are aggressive. Others are what Freud termed sexual, using the word for all pleasure-inducing physiological activities—eating, sleeping and elimination as well as sex. The id seeks immediate gratification without regard for consequences.

The second mental subdivision to develop is the ego. Ideally it serves as a rational manager, conducting the business of living, enabling a person to function effectively and taking into account the consequences of its activities. As manager, the ego exercises the power of decision; it determines what will or will not be done.

In making decisions, the ego weighs information from the id on the one hand and, on the other hand, from the third and last-formed mental structure, the superego. The superego is conscience. It evaluates urges from the id in the light of reality. The superego acts like an idealistic adviser to a head of government, criticizing courses of action, searching for their implications and estimating the consequences. But, like a governmental adviser, it can only counsel, not direct, action. The decision remains with the ego, which balances urges from the id against consequences predicted by the superego and makes the judgment on what to do. If the id urges a sock on the jaw to silence a pest, the ego may heed the warnings of the superego—violence is evil, fighting is illegal and the blow is likely to be returned—or it may decide the provocation is too great for concern over consequences and let go with a fist.

The ego performs its managerial function in two ways. First, it protects itself against the id's most disruptive demands by using various "defense mechanisms," including repression, the process by which forbidden wishes and feelings are kept unconscious, or beyond ordinary awareness. Second, the ego tries to find ways to gratify some of the id's demands without violating sanctions imposed by the superego.

According to psychoanalytic theory, conflict between id and superego is universal. Every person wants some things that are forbidden by society or are impossible of attainment. A strong ego keeps the contending forces in balance so that they cause no trouble.

Unfortunately, the ego is not always strong. Psychoanalytic thinking holds that it becomes strong only if a child progresses smoothly through three phases of development—the oral, anal and oedipal stages.

In an 18th Century engraving of one of literature's most famous examples of an obsessive-compulsive neurosis, Lady Macbeth perplexes her physician and her lady in waiting as she walks in her sleep while unconsciously trying to cleanse her hands of the "damned spot"—the blood of Duncan, King of Scotland, whom she has helped to murder.

In the oral stage—the first 18 months of life, when most of the infant's interest centers on his mouth and his need for food—his parents may be too strict and ungiving, depriving the child of gratification he needs. Because at this point the infant's mind consists only of the primitive id, he cannot reasonably be expected to tolerate much frustration. If he is forced to accept frustration, his emerging ego may be damaged.

Overstrictness is a hazard at the anal stage too. In this period, from about 18 months to three years, the child is preoccupied with the process of elimination—and the parents with toilet training. If they suppress a child's natural rebelliousness at this restriction on his freedom, it may be harder for him to deal with his aggressive drives later.

The child is even more vulnerable in the oedipal stage—named for the mythological Greek hero Oedipus, who unwittingly killed his father and married his mother. During this period, from three to six years old, the child is sexually drawn to the parent of the opposite sex. The adult must tread a narrow line between responsiveness and rejection; too much of either can cause difficulty later. As psychoanalyst Van Buren Hammett put it: "If the father whose little daughter is having her oedipal crush on him likes it too much, and holds her on his lap too much and caresses her too much or even takes her into bed with him, it is apt to overstimulate her." Led on by his responsiveness, the girl never comes to terms with the fact that she cannot have her father for herself. The same is true of a little boy and his mother. On the other hand, Hammett noted, if the loving behavior of an oedipal-age child makes the parents "so anxious that they can't tolerate it and they're cruelly prohibitive, then it's difficult for the child to grow through this stage." Under these circumstances, a girl may grow up to believe that her sexual wishes are bad and that all men will reject her as her father did.

When, for these or other reasons, childhood development does not go smoothly, the ego proves defective in adulthood. Its defensive measures against the id's demands may be so weak that wishes disapproved by the superego threaten to become conscious. Or its ingenuity may not be up to finding acceptable ways of gratifying the id. That is when psychic conflict gets out of hand and leads to neurotic symptoms.

A symptom, according to the psychodynamic theory of neurosis, has two main functions. It serves as a compromise between the mind's warring factions, the instincts on the one hand and the restraining forces on the other. This it does by gratifying forbidden impulses and punishing them at the same time. But the compromise is poor, because the gratification is only symbolic, while the suffering is real. The second function of a symptom is as a defense that tries to keep id and superego apart;

the symptom disguises the true wish or feeling and keeps it unconscious, so that the individual does not have to confront the underlying conflict. But the defense is not very satisfactory either. The forbidden thought still threatens to erupt into consciousness and thus creates the anxiety that is the hallmark of neurosis.

Symptoms of an unresolved oedipal conflict take infinitely varied forms. For the junior executive who resisted promotions, a childhood fear of competing with his father for his mother's affections had turned into an adult fear of doing better than his father at anything. Thus, his normal wish to succeed conflicted with his fear of punishment if he did. By avoiding promotions, he avoided any chance of outstripping his parent. At the same time, he punished himself for the unconscious wish to compete with his father. He also struck an incidental blow at his father, disappointing him by a mediocre performance in life.

A striking example of oedipal conflict is "The Girl Who Couldn't Stop Eating," as psychoanalyst Robert Lindner titled his account of her case. She succumbed to an uncontrollable urge to fasten a pillow around her middle, and to go on eating binges, at the end of which she was physically ill and her apartment was a shambles of empty cans, torn candy wrappers and gnawed bones. She clung unconsciously to her longing for her father and to a passionate desire to have his child. By fastening a pillow to her stomach and bloating her body with food, she was making a pathetic attempt to simulate pregnancy. Lindner discovered much of this early in his treatment of her, but it was months before he found out why she needed to disguise her normal wish for a child. The discovery came through a slip of the tongue. The patient lay on the couch describing her compulsion to convert a pillow into a fantasized state of pregnancy. "I have to mike a new baby," she said. Then she caught herself, horrified. "My God," she said to Lindner. "Did you hear what I just said?" The name of her father was Mike.

One of the most famous cases of an oedipal conflict was reported in detail by Freud himself and has been evaluated by later psychiatrists—some of whom draw conclusions quite different from Freud's. It concerned a small boy, whom Freud called Little Hans, with a phobia of horses. Freud saw the boy only once but guided the father in treatment that was reported to be successful.

At the age of four, Hans became terrified of going outdoors because he was afraid that a horse might bite him or that a horse might fall and get hurt. These symptoms developed at the height of Hans's oedipal conflict, and Freud believed they resulted from it. The boy had not yet repressed his sexual desire for his mother; he loved to get into bed with her—a privilege she granted much more often than Freud thought she should. Hans talked frankly about the time "when I'm married to Mummy," and he even sought direct sexual gratification from her, taking the occasion of his daily bath to suggest that she touch his penis.

As Freud saw it, Little Hans wanted to be rid of his father to have his mother to himself but feared his father would punish him for his "bad" wishes. The unconscious fear and hatred he felt for a parent he also loved were unacceptable to his conscious mind. He tried to repress these powerful feelings, but his childish ego was barely strong enough to contain them. When they threatened to surface, he developed a defense against them in the form of symptoms revolving around fear of horses.

Equating Hans with a horse may seem farfetched, but Freud did not make up this interpretation out of whole cloth; he deduced it from the boy's behavior. He had seen drivers beating their horses, he had been hurt once while playing at being a horse, and a friend's father had warned him that horses can bite. Hans sometimes frisked about like a colt and once told his father, "I'm a young horse." He also tied an improvised nose bag over his face and played a game of nipping at his father. By pinning his fear on horses, which he could avoid, Hans did not have to be consciously afraid of his father, whose loving company he wanted and could not avoid in any case. His unconscious wish to harm his father was symbolically gratified in two ways. First, he projected his aggressive urges onto horses. In his unconscious, horses stood for himself, and he imagined they would inflict painful bites—not on his father (that thought would have been too scary) but on himself. The shift from the father to the son as the person to be bitten came about by a defensive mental process called displacement. It spared Hans a frightening idea—and also punished him symbolically for his murderous wishes.

The principles Freud used in his analysis are widely accepted. Most people recognize instances of projection, in which an individual ascribes to someone else feelings he cannot acknowledge in himself; in Hans's case, for example, aggression was ascribed to horses. Displacement, too, is common; often an individual unconsciously transfers to himself consequences he cannot admit belong to another. But the question of whether these processes were really at work in Hans—and were set off by oedipal conflict—is a subject of controversy. The dispute transcends the case of Hans, for it illustrates the views of those who believe that experiences in the outside world, not inner conflicts, cause neurosis.

Perhaps because this social learning theory of the cause of neurosis is much simpler than the psychodynamic theory, its popularity is grow-

Dramatic insights
to an age of anxiety

*Author-psychologist Rollo May attributes
the current prevalence of anxiety
to a widespread decline of the old values.*

In one stage version of Death of a Salesman, a distraught Willy Loman ponders his failure as his wife and sons look on hopelessly.

More and more people are complaining to psychiatrists and psychologists that they feel unhappy and unfulfilled. Surprisingly (in view of what has been widely believed by experts) many of them find that their troubles cannot be traced to childhood frustrations or festering Freudian wounds.

Increasing numbers of psychiatrists and philosophers are blaming the malaise on the quality of existence itself. The emptiness and uncertainty of people's lives underlie much of neurotic behavior, they say. A leading exponent of this view is psychologist-author Rollo May, who believes the root of the problem is the disappearance of the values people used to live by. May cites Willy Loman in Arthur Miller's play *Death of a Salesman* as an example. Failing at his job, Loman becomes deeply disturbed and ultimately commits suicide. The trouble, says May, is his preoccupation with success.

But May believes more valid values are emerging. He sees a good example in Samuel Beckett's *Waiting for Godot*, in which two tramps, Vladimir and Estragon, support each other while waiting together in an empty world for something to happen. May believes such support will enable man to survive.

Joined in fellowship, Vladimir and Estragon gaze heavenward in Waiting for Godot.

ing in the United States and in Western Europe; it has always been emphasized in the Soviet Union. The basic ideas behind the theory come not from psychoanalysis but from laboratory experiments begun around the turn of the century by Ivan Pavlov on animal responses, and since extended to humans by E. L. Thorndike, John Watson and B. F. Skinner. In this view, neurosis is no more than a destructive habit, or a collection of them, learned by conditioning in about the same way the dogs trained by Pavlov learned to salivate at the sound of a bell. In contrast to the psychodynamic theorist, who sees a symptom as a *sign* of neurosis, the social learning theorist believes the symptom *is* the neurosis.

The phobia of Little Hans has been reinterpreted by two theorists of the social learning school, Joseph Wolpe and Stanley Rachman, who believe it had nothing to do with the boy's father and was, quite simply, an extreme but plausible fear of horses. They pointed out that the boy's fear of horses first appeared when he was walking with his mother and saw a horse fall. Freud had believed that Hans's neurotic conflict over hating and fearing his father existed before this incident and just expressed itself from then on in a horse phobia—in short, that the event precipitated the boy's symptoms but did not cause his neurosis. But to Wolpe and Rachman, the episode was "the cause of the entire disorder," and any inner conflict Hans might have had was irrelevant.

Hans, they suggested, learned to be afraid of horses by "classical" conditioning: horses and fear had become associated in his mind by what he had seen, felt and heard about the harm that horses could cause. The horse's fall on the crucial day finished the conditioning process and finally drove home the lesson that horses are frightening. After that day, said Wolpe and Rachman, Hans's phobia was maintained by "operant" conditioning: every time he avoided an encounter with a horse, he was rewarded by a lessening of his anxiety.

How a therapist treats a patient's neurosis depends on his ideas about what caused the trouble. If he supports the social learning theory of causation, he will employ one of the so-called action therapies, focusing on the neurotic symptoms alone and trying to eliminate them by some technique of behavior modification—conditioning that helps the patient learn to break his unwanted habits. If the therapist supports the psychodynamic theory, he will employ one of the insight treatments, to try to find the underlying meaning and source of the symptoms, and thus resolve the conflicts that presumably cause them.

Psychoanalysis is the archetype of the insight therapies. The basic aim is, in psychiatrist Karl Menninger's words, to "change the structure of a patient's mind"—to redevelop those parts of his personality harmed by the unresolved conflicts. To expose the repressed fantasies, fears and wishes, the analyst tries to help the patient recapture the events of his childhood and his buried feelings about them. In the light of grown-up rationality, ancient terrors can be dismissed when they are seen to be based on fantasied or long-past dangers; infantile wishes can be renounced when they are recognized as impossible to fulfill.

Innumerable cartoons poke fun at the setup of a typical session in psychoanalysis: the patient lies on a couch, rambling on, while out of his sight sits the analyst. But there are reasons for this arrangement, developed by Freud himself. Lying on a couch relaxes the patient physically and helps him discuss topics that arouse anxiety in him. The analyst sits where the patient cannot see in order to limit the patient's visual stimuli and to create an atmosphere of total objectivity. He keeps silent, usually breaking in only when a point of particular significance arises, so the patient will be otherwise uninterrupted in following the basic rule of analysis: to say what comes to mind, no matter how irrelevant, trivial, impolite, unconventional or humiliating it may seem.

Often the patient puts up unconscious defenses against letting repressed ideas surface; in this case interpretation of his dreams may overcome the resistance. Psychoanalysis attaches enormous importance to dreams. Lawrence Kubie noted: "Although every dream starts from an unhappy residue of trivial current experiences, each represents a condensation of our past." Sometimes, however, a dream is so repugnant to a patient that it only stiffens his resistance and may even block treatment. Karl Menninger told of a handsome young man who sought analysis because of his unsatisfying sex life. At first he talked freely. Then, between sessions, he dreamed of exploring a house and finding something in a dark corner that made him recoil in horror. It was, he reported to Menninger, "too awful to look at. Perhaps it was a decaying dog—a cur—a beast—something of mine." In the dream, he rushed from the building—and a few days later from treatment as well, writing Menninger that he did not believe he needed analysis after all. He could not, in fact, face up to it.

At the heart of the psychoanalytic process is the phenomenon known as transference. In time the patient reacts to his analyst as if the physician were his parent. Unconsciously, he ascribes to the analyst characteristics of his parents, and reexperiences all the feelings—love, hate, fear, envy, distrust—that these qualities evoked in him when he was little. Transference occurs in many ordinary relationships; an employee, for instance, may unconsciously equate his boss with his father

—even though his father was harsh and his boss is genial—and rebel against his boss with self-destructive results. In daily life such transference may go unnoticed; in analysis it is carefully studied. The analyst, interpreting the patient's attitudes toward him, helps the patient to see more clearly his often inappropriate patterns of behavior toward other people and demonstrates how conflicts that originated with parents in the past are influencing the patient's life in the present.

To facilitate transference, the analyst tries to maintain his "analytic incognito," revealing as little about himself as possible; that is another reason for his staying out of the patient's sight during sessions. In Kubie's words, the analyst ideally remains "a neutral sample of humanity" and "a peg on which the patient can hang his conscious and unconscious fantasies." Were the relationship between patient and analyst to become less neutral, the patient could claim that the feelings he had transferred to the analyst were based on real facts he knew about the analyst, and he might never learn that transferred feelings were, in fact, warping his relationships with many people.

Psychoanalysis has many critics. It takes a long time, usually two to five years, often more. It costs thousands of dollars. The size of the monetary investment has, in fact, led to a celebrated quip, credited to the British physician and wit, Lord Webb-Johnson. Defining the difference between a neurotic and a psychotic, he described the first as "the man who builds a castle in the air," the second as "the man who lives in it." And, he added, the psychiatrist is "the man who collects the rent."

A perhaps more trenchant criticism of psychoanalysis is that it is unlikely to help a patient unless he can meet several criteria of "analyzability." He must be intelligent, inward-looking, gifted at thinking in psychological terms, not too emotionally sick, and articulate (because words are the medium of treatment).

Because true Freudian psychoanalysis is an elitist therapy, affordable only by the few who are financially and intellectually qualified, most patients now receive treatments that, while still based on the theory of psychoanalysis, are variants of it. They are less costly, less lengthy and less intensive. One method, called brief psychotherapy, requires as little as one weekly session for a year or less, each session lasting 15 or 20 minutes as opposed to the 45 or 60 minutes of psychoanalytic sessions. The aim is not to restructure the patient's entire personality but to focus on immediate problems. No couch awaits the patient; he talks to the therapist eye to eye, usually across a desk. The therapist does not remain silent or aloof. Instead, he takes a positive role, offering specific suggestions for relieving the patient's dilemma.

Positive guidance by the therapist also characterizes other psychotherapies. In the various kinds of group therapy that have become popular, the therapist serves as group leader, stimulating discussion and encouraging interaction. In family therapy, the therapist first deals with the individual as the "primary" patient, then meets with the family as a unit, often visiting their home to observe conflicts firsthand.

How well any of the psychotherapies, or psychoanalysis itself, works is a subject of continuing, often acrimonious, debate. In 1952 a British psychologist who is a sharp critic of Freudian methods, Hans Eysenck, touched off a furor when he suggested that untreated neurotics recover as often as those who undergo psychoanalysis or psychotherapy. Eysenck analyzed 24 studies that reported improvement and recovery rates for more than 8,000 neurotic patients. He calculated that 44 per cent of the neurotics treated by psychoanalysis were either improved or cured at the end of treatment. For 7,293 patients treated by other methods, he judged the rate of improvement or cure to be 64 per cent.

In a recent reanalysis of Eysenck's cases, psychologist Allen Bergin

Freud's own couch, the rug-covered prototype of the principal prop of psychoanalysis, dominates a comfortable consulting room that displays Near Eastern sculptures (foreground) he collected. Freud insisted that patients lie down, facing away from him, because he believed they then could more easily relax and reveal underlying feelings.

concluded that the facts in the 24 studies used by Eysenck were so ambiguous that the controversy over his conclusion could never be resolved. Bergin's own survey of newer studies indicated that as many as 30 per cent of neurotics may improve spontaneously, while about 65 per cent improve if treated. However, these later studies were also imprecise, Bergin cautioned. Taking possible errors into account, he reported, "there remains some modest evidence that psychotherapy works." The statement was one that could comfort proponents of either side of the controversy—depending on how they defined "modest evidence."

Freud himself once suggested that psychoanalysis would in time become more important as a science of the unconscious than as a therapeutic procedure, and his prediction is being borne out not only by the increasing use of less time-consuming psychotherapies but also by the rising interest—in both the United States and Europe—in therapies based on the social learning theory of the cause of neurosis. All employ techniques to help a patient unlearn symptoms he has previously learned by experience or to teach him new ways of behaving that are incompatible with his old neurotic ways.

To treat Little Hans, for example, a behavior therapist probably would have used the method called systematic desensitization. Since Hans's fear of horses had led him to fear going outdoors, various inducements would retrain him, bit by bit, to connect going outdoors with pleasurable, nonthreatening activities, such as going to buy pastry. His sensitivity to outdoor dangers would be systematically reduced.

This technique, pioneered by Dr. Joseph Wolpe of Temple University Medical Center, has been applied to cure a number of phobias. Someone who is terrified of flying begins with a series of exercises that teach him how to relax hands and arms, then face and shoulders, trunk and abdomen, thighs, legs, feet and finally the whole body. Meanwhile, therapist and patient consider the separate situations that stir up the phobia, arranging them in a kind of hierarchy. At the bottom may be such matters as deciding to take a plane trip and buying a ticket; near the top will be going to the airport, taking off, flying and landing; in between may be as many as 50 other anxiety triggers.

The patient is then asked to imagine an innocuous scene such as lying in a hammock. This is intended to calm him and help fend off anxiety. The therapist then describes the least threatening activity in the hierarchy and asks the patient to immerse himself in it in fantasy. If he can manage this without becoming anxious, he is asked to contemplate the next scene in the hierarchy; if he cannot, he is told to imagine himself back in the hammock, and the therapist moves back a rung on

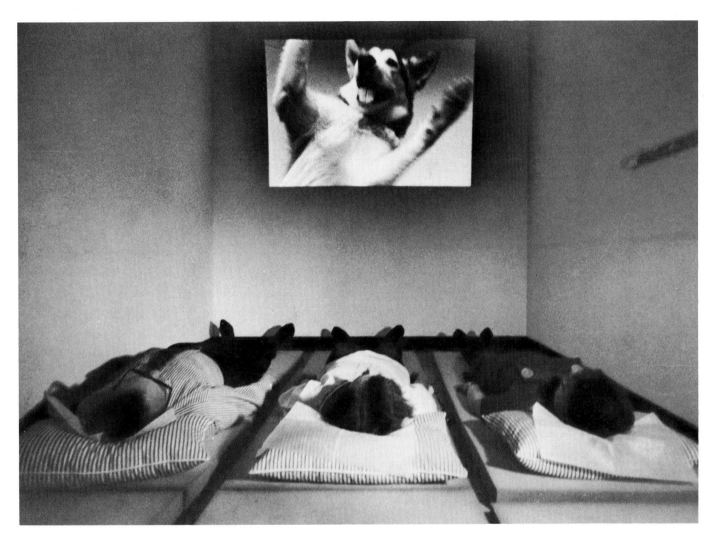

A lunging German shepherd projected from a slide looms above three young people, participants in step-by-step behavior therapy that seeks to rid them of their neurotic fear of dogs. First they look at photographs of small animals; then they view larger dogs like this one. Finally they confront real-life animals, pet them and walk them on leashes.

the ladder of anxiety triggers to begin the entire process again. When the patient can imagine the whole list of items in the hierarchy without feeling fear, he can presumably do the same thing in real life.

Another behavior modification technique used to treat phobias is implosion, devised by psychologist Thomas Stampfl of John Carroll University in Ohio. In a sense it is the opposite of systematic desensitization. As psychologist Perry London sums up Stampfl's aims: "He does not want to soothe his patient or gradually increase his tolerance for anxiety by giving it first in small doses, but to terrify him, to shock him, to produce an explosion of panic within him. Thus the name Implosive Therapy, treatment by inward explosion."

The therapist touches off the explosion by describing in detail the situation that most terrifies his patient, then asks him to imagine himself in the midst of it. This quickly produces terrible anxiety in the patient, but he also knows that at the moment he cannot experience any harm, as he fears he might in real life. When the patient is repeatedly subjected to this tormenting but imaginary ordeal, he gradually becomes inured to the therapist's vivid descriptions and his anxiety is extinguished.

Occasionally the therapist exposes the patient to the real thing. A 41-year-old woman developed a phobia of cancer after her father died of the disease, and she came to regard objects that the dead man had touched as carriers of disease. After a while her fears began to center on raw pork, but her phobia spread to so many other things that she could hardly perform any household task whatever.

The therapist took her into a small, windowless room where something lay concealed on a table. Told to remove the covering, the patient did so—and shrank back, sobbing, from a piece of raw pork beside a mound of minced pork. The therapist asked her to touch the meat; she obeyed but stood at arm's length from it. Then the therapist made a meatball from the minced pork and threw it to her. She caught it, and they tossed it back and forth. "I know you hope this will disintegrate and spatter all over me," the patient said. Exactly that happened. After further sessions, her fears diminished and she was able to function again.

A number of other behavior modification techniques are basically modern variants of old-fashioned training methods: aversion therapy is mild punishment (nausea-causing pills) to deter unwanted habits; positive reinforcement is rewards (praise, extra privileges, money) to encourage wanted habits; modeling is imitation (the therapist may demonstrate behavior the patient fears doing, and the patient is led to copy it). In a comparison of several techniques, psychologist Albert T. Bandura of Stanford University tested people who suffered from a phobia of snakes. Bandura divided his subjects into four groups. One got no therapy and was used as a control to measure the impact of treatment on the others. Of the three treated groups, one was given systematic desensitization. The second learned special relaxation exercises, then viewed a film on snake handling. The third group watched the therapist caress a real snake of formidable proportions and drape it around his neck; then each member of the group took a turn at doing the same. All three groups lost much of their fear of snakes, but those who had modeled their behavior on the therapist's emerged the bravest.

Most applications of these methods have concentrated on clear-cut phobias—a single type of unwanted behavior that could be attacked directly. But more recently success has been claimed for behaviorist treatment of the more complex and generalized ailments, such as anxiety neurosis. G. Terence Wilson of Rutgers and Gerald Davison of Stony Brook University described the case of a young librarian who suffered from insomnia and tension headaches, felt anxious and depressed, lacked confidence in herself and was unable to relate sexually to her husband. Her symptoms appeared so generalized—"I guess I'm just an uptight person," she said—that her therapist asked her to keep a diary to try to pin down what was troubling her. The therapist singled out three problem areas to treat. He prescribed relaxation training that taught her how to relax and tighten muscles systematically; he showed her, by encouragement and modeling, how to be more self-assertive and overcome her feelings of worthlessness; and finally he enrolled her with her husband in a program of sexual training. Four months later she felt well enough to take a university course for an advanced degree.

Such behavior modification techniques are often criticized on philosophical grounds. The insight therapist believes that each human being is responsible for his own behavior, and he tries to strengthen his patient so he can manage his life as he sees fit. The behaviorist takes on himself the responsibility for another person's manner of acting; in effect, he *makes* a patient act in a certain way by imposing controls from outside. Judd Marmor, a well-known Los Angeles psychoanalyst, noted that this kind of treatment comes "uncomfortably close to the dangerous area of thought and behavior control."

Neither type of treatment for neuroses seems to have a clear advantage over the other. There is no objective measurement of improvement or cure. In one of the more balanced studies, Lester Luborsky of the University of Pennsylvania found that "in most of the comparisons of behavior therapy with other psychotherapies, the differences in the amount of benefits they provide for patients are not significant." Basing his findings on 19 studies, he found that behavior therapy emerged as superior to other psychotherapies in only six comparisons; and these six he criticized for being of poor research quality or based on too brief a period of time to make a fair evaluation. More important than making a final judgment on either treatment, in the opinion of many psychiatrists, is matching the patient with the form of therapy that will work better for him. Most patients would agree with this view.

The recovered neurotic himself needs no objective tests to prove he is well. He knows, and the people around him often know it too and comment on how different he seems. His life is frequently transformed. His inhibitions, not just sexual but creative, have loosened. His capacity to experience pleasure—and to endure physical and mental suffering when necessary—has deepened. He is no longer "at war with himself," in Freud's phrase; he has gained a large measure of peace.

The Depths of Despair

3

In western Nigeria, an energetic Yoruba woman gradually withdraws from village life, ceases tending her garden, and—to the dismay of her family and neighbors—spends her days staring at the walls of her hut. In Osaka, Japan, a conscientious college student suffers weeks of anxiety and shame, convinced he will fail an upcoming examination, and prepares to disembowel himself. In Southern California, a hard-driving sales manager repeatedly cancels important appointments, lets his paper work pile up and indulges in cocktails until past midnight.

Separated by vast distances, these three individuals could hardly be more unlike in cultural experience, social background and way of life. Emotionally, however, the disconsolate African mother, the suicidal Japanese youth and the procrastinating American businessman resemble one another more closely than they do their own kin. Their outlook is clouded by fear, dread, unhappiness and self-dislike, and they feel no hope that they will recapture past joys and satisfactions. Their common bond is depression, a mental state that can affect anyone, anywhere.

Just about everyone knows occasional feelings of mild depression —hours or days that bring to the lips such expressions as "I'm miserable," "I can't concentrate" or "What's the use?" Add a downcast expression, a slowed gait and a slumped posture, and the picture of a bout of "the blues" is complete. At these times, the laundry tends to go unwashed, bills remain unpaid and the most compelling urge is to take to bed and pull up the covers. Such low periods come to even the staunchest optimist at times, but they are a problem only if they persist.

Almost everyone also suffers periods of deeper depression, the reaction to some shattering event—the death of a parent, the loss of a job or serious bodily injury. The despair can be so black that treatment is called for, but in most cases time and sympathy enable the sufferer to work out his feelings of grief and loss, adjust to the changed circumstances and resume the business of living.

In millions of people, however, depression occurs for no apparent reason. It can range from mild to severe, and it can linger for many months or even years. Negative feelings dominate all aspects of living and, in the most severe cases, can lead to hallucinations, withdrawal from all activities and complete breakdown, physical as well as mental. Such depressions constitute a debilitating sickness that, according to the American psychiatrist Hugh Storrow, "probably causes more human suffering than any other single disease—mental or physical."

Sometimes referred to whimsically as the common cold of mental illness, depression actually exacts a social cost far greater than does the ubiquitous grippe. It is the prime cause of admission to mental hospitals in Britain and ranks second only to schizophrenia in filling mental wards in the United States. The World Health Organization estimates that one of every five persons in the technically advanced countries experiences depression, and it is on the rise in rapidly changing underdeveloped countries, among them Ghana, Nigeria and Ethiopia. Depression paves the way for drug abuse, especially of amphetamines and other drugs that induce excitement—a "high" to counteract the low of depression. It is a precursor to alcoholism for millions of people. And because 75 per cent of all suicide attempts are attributable to depression, it is, in Storrow's words, "one of the few psychiatric illnesses with a significant mortality rate."

Fortunately, with increased awareness of the wide reach of depression, there has been steady progress toward understanding its origins, nature and cure. It has come to be viewed as a complex malady in which both psychological and biochemical factors may figure, abetted by environmental and in some cases perhaps genetic influences. But, according to two leading authorities on the subject, psychiatrists Frederic F. Flach and Suzanne C. Draghi, depression is now regarded as "definable, recognizable, treatable, and in a real sense, preventable." The most encouraging advance is the development of drugs that, supported by some form of psychotherapy, can bring complete recovery in virtually every case.

Depression is no newcomer to the list of human woes. The Bible contains numerous vivid accounts of the affliction. Any modern sufferer would empathize with the patriarch Job, who, stripped of health, wealth and family as a test of his faith in God, lamented: "Why didst thou bring me forth from the womb? Would that I had died before any eye had seen me. . . . My face is red with weeping, and on my eyelids is deep darkness. . . . Where then is my hope?"

Ancient Greeks, too, were well acquainted with the illness. It was Hippocrates, the "father of medicine," who 2,400 years ago rightly identified depression as a disease of the mind. The pragmatic Greek healer theorized that the cause was an imbalance of bodily fluids—specifically an excess of "black bile," in Greek, *melan cholē* (hence melancholia, the term for depression until the start of this century). Though the theory was wrong, Hippocrates hit upon an effective treatment. He and his fellow healers sent disturbed patients to take the soothing waters at a warm mineral spring in Italy. As it happened, the spring was rich in lithium, a metallic element that modern medicine has only recently discovered as effective in treating depression.

As usual, Hippocrates was well ahead of his time. For many centuries thereafter most physicians, churchmen and laymen regarded melancholia as divine punishment for moral transgressions. Martin Luther flatly pronounced it "the work of the devil." The 17th Century English writer Robert Burton, the most assiduous student of depression of his day, believed its primary cause was original sin—the taint of sin that, according to Christian belief, all human beings are born with. Burton was himself a melancholic, and he devoted a lifetime to preparing *The Anatomy of Melancholy*, a compendium of lore on the subject, including anecdotes and psychological and philosophical observations. For all its archaic language, Burton's description of the melancholic is still apt: an individual who suffers anguish "without a fever, having for his ordinary companions fear and sadness, without any apparent occasion." Burton also neatly presaged those psychoanalysts who theorize that depression is attributable to childhood traumas; he laid part of the blame on parents, who "cause our grief many times."

History records moments when depression was even a fashionable ailment. Queen Elizabeth's courtiers boasted of their despair, deeming it a sign of refined sensitivity. When they went to the theater they found a kindred spirit in Shakespeare's "melancholy Dane," Hamlet. In the late 18th Century, Goethe's novel *The Sorrows of Young Werther* took Europe by storm. Its hero, a breast-beating failure in love as well as in his idealistic ambitions, sums up his plight thus: "God knows, I lie down to sleep so often with the wish, sometimes with the hope, that I shall not wake again." This hope unrealized, Werther blows his brains out—a solution so persuasive to Goethe's readers that it set off a wave of actual suicides among young German romantics.

Perhaps depression has acquired a certain chic because it has frequently struck notable personages. Many of them over the centuries have disregarded the customary taboo on discussion of emotional ills and have freely admitted their affliction. Abraham Lincoln endured such low periods that he suspected he might kill himself during one of these sieges and so, unlike most young Americans of his day, would not even carry a pocketknife. Sigmund Freud was melancholic as a young man and experimented with cocaine as a treatment until he learned that the drug was habit-forming. Winston Churchill suffered recurrent spells of the illness and referred to it, with typical Churchillian flair for the picturesque, as his "black dog." Such literary figures as Nathaniel Hawthorne and Edgar Allen Poe were on the roster of depressives, and the illness led to the suicides of two of this century's most brilliant women—poet Sylvia Plath and novelist Virginia Woolf.

Though depression can befall anyone, certain categories of people are apparently more vulnerable than others. Notably, various studies suggest that it occurs more often in women than in men and more often in married than in single people. One estimate indicates that three times as many women as men experience depression, but no one is sure why. Some experts speculate that hormonal differences may be to blame; some conjecture that women are under increasing strain because of the growing issue of their role in society. Other authorities, however, challenge the estimate itself. Myrna Weissman, professor of psychiatry at Yale University, noted that men are generally more reluctant to acknowledge depression, and are more likely to mask it with alcohol. Statistics seem to bolster this view; the alcoholism rate is four times higher among men than women.

Attempts at suicide, the tragic culmination of many depressions, also reveal some sex differences. Four times as many women as men try suicide, but three times as many men succeed. Women usually opt for pills or gas; either method leaves time for a rescue. Men choose routes to self-extinction less easy to block—guns, nooses or leaps from tall buildings.

Why more married than unmarried people are prey to depression —a ratio not found in any other psychiatric illness—is explained with a fair degree of unanimity by investigators. A major cause of depression is the failure of a close relationship that involves the affections. The relationship does not have to be marital. But, as psychiatrist Mortimer Ostow put it, marriage "constitutes the primary vehicle for the expression of responsibility and the need to love, care, and protect others." If the vehicle breaks down—as a result, for example, of sexual mismatching, or the excessive dependence of one partner, or strains that arise in the course of aging—depression is often the outcome.

Until recently, any adult—married or single—was thought to be far more likely than any youngster to experience depression; it was, indeed, considered a misfortune virtually exclusive to grownups. But it is

continued on page 73

A shy and hauntingly lovely young woman, Virginia Woolf was photographed at the age of 20 with her stern Victorian father, Leslie Stephen, a prosperous editor. In a novel, she portrayed him as "petty, selfish, vain and egotistical," but his death, two years after this picture was taken, brought on her second collapse.

A famous tragedy of depression

In the spring of 1941, the English novelist Virginia Woolf sat down in her house in the Sussex village of Rodmell and wrote a letter to her husband, Leonard. "Dearest," she said, "I feel certain I am going mad again. I feel we can't go through another of those terrible times. And I shan't recover this time." She placed the letter on the mantelpiece and walked out across the meadow to the River Ouse. Then she stuffed a heavy stone into her coat pocket, plunged into the river and drowned.

Woolf's suicide was the culmination of one of the most famous cases of manic depression, and its course typifies the severe form of this illness. Family background provided the setting, lifetime experiences favored depression, and a brilliant woman's responses were al-

most predictable. "She became painfully excitable and then intolerably depressed," wrote her biographer and nephew, Quentin Bell. She collapsed when her mother died in 1895 and again at her father's death nine years later. She attempted suicide in 1913 and a little over a year later was reduced to babbling incoherence, talking with imaginary birds in Greek and carrying on conversations with her dead mother.

Somehow, in between episodes of mental illness, she managed to write some of the most beautiful prose in all of English literature in novels such as *Jacob's Room, Mrs. Dalloway* and *To the Lighthouse.* Finally, when she heard "horrible voices" and sensed the onset of another, and perhaps irreversible attack, she could fight no more.

Virginia's ill-starred family gathered for a portrait in 1893. Included are her mother (top row center), who died when Virginia was 13, and George Duckworth (top row, white hat), whose sexual advances terrified Virginia. Virginia sits at front row center, with her beautiful sister Vanessa, whom she admired but envied, at far left. Brother Thoby, whose death at 26 devastated both girls, is second from the left.

Virginia Woolf was raised in an environment that seemed to guarantee mental instability. A stepsister and a cousin were psychotics confined in institutions. The deaths of her mother, father, beloved stepsister and a brother were disastrous shocks. A stepbrother molested her when she was six. Although other men pursued her in adult life, she was frigid and her marriage was characterized by intellectual companionship rather than by passion. Even during her married years her strongest emotional attachments were with women, but her biographer Quentin Bell did not believe that she was overtly homosexual.

Virginia embraces one of her great passions, six-foot-tall Violet Dickinson, a family friend, in a photograph made in 1902.

Brother-in-law Clive Bell, watching his son Julian play with Virginia, pursued her after marrying her sister Vanessa.

Virginia (left) and her great love, the bisexual Vita Sackville-West, are pictured with Vita's two sons.

Husband Leonard, shown with Virginia after their marriage in 1912, was a brilliant man who protected his fragile wife.

*In a gloomy portrait made two years before her suicide,
a haggard Virginia Woolf exudes depression. "Death," said her
husband, "was part of the deep imbalance of her mind."*

now known to be a major health threat among adolescents as well. In Britain, for example, a rising rate of suicide attempts by the young accounts currently for 20 per cent of all emergency-room cases. Even the very young, it has come to be recognized, manifest symptoms associated with depression. Infants in orphanages—deprived of the affectionate physical and emotional contact involved in mothering—are subject to depressive withdrawals. They refuse to eat, appear sad and listless, and fail to develop normal motor and speech skills. In some cases, the withdrawal is so acute that the infant dies.

Along with dispatching the myth that depression is related to age, researchers have pretty much demolished the notion that it is, in one investigator's words, "an upper-class malady." In some respects, the opposite is true. People at the lower economic levels are more likely to suffer severe forms of depression. At the same time, they are less likely to be accurately diagnosed—at least initially because even among doctors, the belief in depression as an elite ailment dies hard. Evidence to this effect was uncovered by a University of Florida psychiatric team investigating medical patients at a local hospital. Physicians there, when asked by the researchers to make a tentative diagnosis of the subjects, detected depression in four times as many upper-class as lower-class patients. In sharp contrast, when the researchers themselves rated the patients on a scale of common symptoms of depression, they found the disorder more than twice as prevalent in the less affluent group.

Recognizing depression poses a challenge even to specialists, not only because it takes various forms but also because certain symptoms—crying jags, for instance, or sleeplessness, or loss of appetite—can apply with equal validity to mild, neurotic depressions that impair some of an individual's capacities and to severe psychotic depressions.

The American Psychiatric Association's guidelines distinguish between two basic types of depressive disorders: those that are affective, or endogenous, that is, internally caused, not sparked by any external incident; and those that are reactive, responses to some overt stress situation. Generally speaking, endogenous depression is more severe and longer lasting, and it is psychotic—the patient is so deeply disturbed he loses contact with reality. Reactive depression, too, can be psychotic, but more often it is neurotic—the victim understands the reasons for his sadness, and he remains rational. Reactive depression, whether psychotic or neurotic, is of relatively short duration, usually ending when there is an improvement in the stress situation that brought it on.

Defining a stress situation, however, can be a very tricky matter, for a number of reasons. Generalizing is risky because, as one researcher observed, "One man's stress situation is another man's shrug of the shoulders." Not only do two individuals vary in their reactions when faced with comparable adverse circumstances, but each individual responds differently to different troubles of his own. The loss of a person's pet collie may depress him and the loss of a friend may not. If a hurricane ravages his beach property, he may view the damages to his cottage with calm but feel inconsolable about his wrecked sailboat. His degree of attachment to whatever is lost, not the objective worth of the loss, determines the severity and extent of his depressive reaction.

A severe stress situation can induce reactive depression that is psychotic in nature. The illness not only entails greatly intensified negative feelings but also leads to hallucinations and delusions. One case involved a 21-year-old infantryman. He was handling a loaded carbine when it discharged and killed a friend. Court-martialed and sent to prison, the infantryman underwent a complete psychotic breakdown. He wept violently and tried to hang himself with his pajamas and to slash his wrists. Until treatment ultimately enabled him to live with his guilt, he hallucinated long conversations in which the dead man alternately urged him to commit suicide and to keep on living.

In reactive depressions of the neurotic kind, the stress situation evokes a less spectacular but still tormenting response in even the healthiest psychological specimen. A case in point is Colonel Edwin E. "Buzz" Aldrin Jr., the second man to walk on the moon. Like all the other astronauts, Aldrin was subjected in advance to the most thorough evaluation for psychological fitness ever devised for any human being. Neither the intensive preparation nor the execution of the Apollo 11 flight produced serious emotional strain. But the subsequent public adulation, goodwill tours and speaking engagements did. In his autobiography, *Return to Earth*, Aldrin recalled that he began to experience a progressive loss of confidence and self-esteem until, as he put it, "I stopped. Stopped everything. I'd go to my office in the morning, determined to work a full day and then go home to more work. I'd sit down at my desk and stare out the window. A few hours would go by and I'd drive to the beach. . . . Then I'd go home for dinner, turn on the television, and get a bottle of Scotch. Or I'd not go home at all until everyone was in bed." Early in the illness, Aldrin had crying spells after some speaking engagements; later he developed physical symptoms, such as a painful neck and numbed fingers. His recovery came after he had received both antidepressant medication and psychotherapy.

Aldrin's ordeal was a perfect example of what psychiatrists call a postachievement depression—a kind of reactive depression brought on,

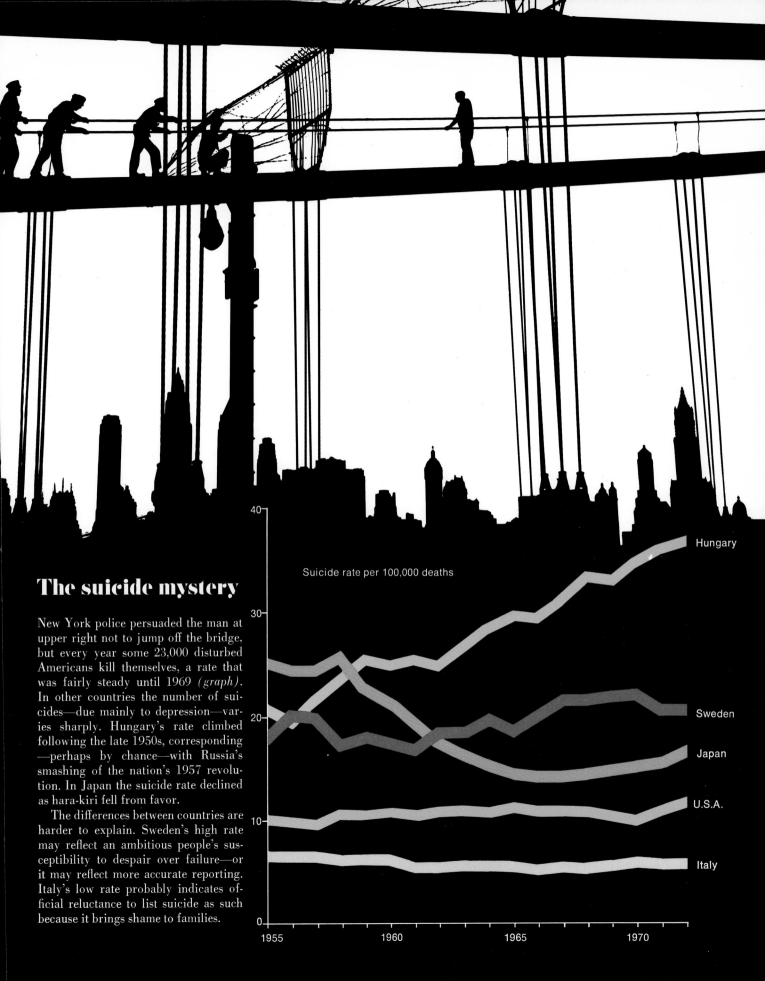

The suicide mystery

New York police persuaded the man at upper right not to jump off the bridge, but every year some 23,000 disturbed Americans kill themselves, a rate that was fairly steady until 1969 *(graph)*. In other countries the number of suicides—due mainly to depression—varies sharply. Hungary's rate climbed following the late 1950s, corresponding —perhaps by chance—with Russia's smashing of the nation's 1957 revolution. In Japan the suicide rate declined as hara-kiri fell from favor.

The differences between countries are harder to explain. Sweden's high rate may reflect an ambitious people's susceptibility to despair over failure—or it may reflect more accurate reporting. Italy's low rate probably indicates official reluctance to list suicide as such because it brings shame to families.

Suicide rate per 100,000 deaths

Hungary

Sweden

Japan

U.S.A.

Italy

40

30

20

10

0

1955   1960   1965   1970

paradoxically, by success. In theory, someone who reaches a desired goal should feel gratified. In practice, many people find that "it is better to travel than to arrive," as the old adage says. A political candidate wins high office after a strenuous campaign for the post, then realizes that he fears the responsibilities that go with it. An author produces a bestseller but worries that the next book will prove a flop. An industrialist who has built a fortune on his ability to make quick judgments turns increasingly indecisive. Whatever rewards success brings, depression may still follow. One cause, studies show, is a loss of the stimulus that drove the achiever toward his goal; another is a dread of not sustaining the achievement.

However painful reactive depressions may be to their victims, the fact that they can be traced to some external event or circumstance is of obvious help in dealing with them. But in the other basic category of depression, the endogenous kind—originating from within—the clues are hidden deep inside the individual and are much less easy to track down.

The best-known type of endogenous depression, so-called manic depression, is perhaps the most baffling, because the victim is not consistently depressed. Instead, he experiences dramatic swings in mood, alternating between despair and elation. In the depressed period, he feels hopeless, lonely, full of dread and foreboding; in the manic stage, he feels irrationally exhilarated, hyperactive, able to cope with anything.

One famous victim of manic depression, Joshua Logan, the producer-director of *South Pacific* and other theatrical hits, vividly described the effects of his sickness. During his manic phase, Logan recalled, "I would be going great guns, putting out a thousand ideas a minute, acting flamboyant—until I went over the bounds of reality." Then his mood would plummet, leaving him with the "wish to be dead without having to go through the shaming defeat of suicide." Though the agony of depression was terrible, Logan noted, "elation, its nonidentical twin sister, is even more terrifying—attractive as she may be for a moment. You are grandiose beyond the reality of your creativity."

The causes of reactive depression are comparatively easy to find, but the origins of endogenous depressions of the sort that troubled Joshua Logan have remained, until the 20th Century, largely a mystery. The modern clues began to appear early in the century, when Freud developed the ideas of Karl Abraham, a German psychoanalyst who had noticed that the attitudes of depressed people were similar to those of people actually grieving over the deaths of relatives or friends. Both,

Freud suggested, were suffering the loss of a "love object," but the mourner's lost object was identifiable while the depressed person's was not—the feelings of loss were unfocused. Both also developed feelings of hostility, but again there was a difference. The mourner unconsciously felt angry at the dead person, but the depressed person directed these feelings toward himself—"anger turned inward." Freud pursued the theme in a now-classic paper, "Mourning and Melancholia," published in 1917. Mourning, he theorized, is the process that enables an individual gradually to detach himself from the lost love object, working out guilt and anger by consciously recalling—and fantasizing about—the deceased. With these activities, the intense emotional bond to the lost person loosens and eventually the mourner turns to new interests, freed from his grief.

On the other hand, Freud noted, the depressed individual does not get over his feelings of loss, anger and guilt. He completely loses sight of the lost love object and turns these feelings solely upon himself—with a vengeance. "We see that the ego debases itself and rages against itself," Freud wrote, adding, "and as little as the patient do we understand what this can lead to and how it can change."

Freud thought that the lost love object of the depressed person could be either another person, or a homeland or even an intangible ideal. Abraham later suggested another type of loss—the withdrawal of love from an infant during the oral stage. This trauma, Abraham argued, could condition an individual for depressive episodes in adult life. Psychoanalytic theorists such as Melanie Klein and Therese Benedeck subsequently amplified this view, suggesting that infantile feelings of frustration and anger could create in an individual a predisposition toward depression.

The psychoanalytic theory of the origin of depression held sway for so long that when the first pragmatic remedy for the malady was found in the 1930s, it was believed to work because it affected the human unconscious. In this procedure, commonly called shock treatment, chemical injections and eventually mild electrical currents were used to jolt the brain. The electrical treatment, technically known as electroconvulsive therapy (ECT), proved very effective. It provided dramatic relief to patients judged to be hopelessly in the grip of severe depression; after six to eight treatments, 80 per cent of the patients were completely cured. The only discernible side effect was temporary confusion or memory loss. Attempting to explain the efficacy of the therapy, psychiatrists speculated that the unconscious accepted the electric shocks as a punishment that expiated the guilt at the core of the depression.

In oppression, the birth of the blues

"They were songs that sprang from troubled minds, songs that reflected anxiety and agitation, guilt feelings, hunger, depression and occasionally the joys of momentary release from a burdened life"—that is how British musicologist Leonard Feather described the blues, the unique music born in the mental anguish of blacks in the American South in the late 19th Century.

The origins of the blues can be traced to African music and even to European ballads, but the main roots lie in the work songs of Southern prisoners and the field chants of cotton pickers.

In the standard blues form, haunting melodies support lyrics made up of three-line stanzas in which the first line is always repeated. Some stanzas are generalized laments, as in the first three lines of "Sunrise Blues" below. But many are about specific miseries—prison, lynchings or most frequently, unrequited love.

The names of the people who composed most of these songs have long since been lost, but their works continue to live on through the recordings of the artists who popularized this remarkable music.

The singers who made the records at left—Bertha "Chippie" Smith, Ida Cox and the legendary Bessie Smith— were numbered among the most talented of the popularizers of the blues.

I had the blues before sunrise, with tears standing in my eyes,
I had the blues before sunrise, with tears standing in my eyes,
It's such a miserable feeling, a feelin' that I feel despised.

Seems like everybody, everybody's down on me,
Seems like everybody, everybody's down on me,
I'm gonna cast my troubles, down in the deep blue sea.

Blues start to roll in, and stop at my front door,
Blues start to roll in, and stop at my front door,
I'm gonna change my way of living, ain't gonna worry no more.

Now, I love my baby, but my baby won't behave,
Now, I love my baby, but my baby won't behave,
I'm gonna buy me a sharp shootin' pistol, and put her in her grave.

But in the early 1960s a Swedish psychiatrist, Gunnar Karl Holmberg, demonstrated that shock causes significant biological changes in the body, increasing the concentration of various chemicals in the blood. Such bodily changes could not be tied directly to the alleviation of depression. However, later experiments, which indicate a link between depression and chemicals in the brain itself, raised the possibility that shock may work its miracles through its effects on tangible tissue rather than on the intangible unconscious.

While some scientists attempt to unravel the intricate relationship between biochemical imbalances and depression, others pursue the possibility that genetic inheritance also may contribute to the making of a melancholic individual. Studies of depression in identical twins, who possess identical genes, suggest that there may be a hereditary predisposition to the illness. But the problems of collecting evidence —finding identical twins victimized by depression, then untangling the complex influences of environment—make proof of genetic involvement very difficult. One leading authority, Aaron T. Beck, professor of psychiatry at the University of Pennsylvania, noted: "The available research data does not establish conclusively whether affective disorders are genetic, environmental, both, or neither."

Paralleling the investigation of hereditary and biochemical factors in depression has been a more extensive search for psychological influences. Freud and his followers had concentrated on the effects of crucial experiences, in childhood and later. More recently, behavioral scientists have taken a broader view of experience, and have considered the depressive effects of almost anything that might interact with an individual during his lifetime—his job, family, surroundings.

Some psychiatrists have turned their attention to physical environment as a potential cause of depression. If an individual's anxiety about his surroundings is deep-seated and unfocused, he may suffer an endogenous depression; on the other hand, his surroundings very often produce the overt stress situations that evoke a reactive depression. This has been a common response among European workers who have had to leave home and go to another country to earn a living.

Dr. Francesco Simone of the psychiatric clinic of the University of Naples found depression—the most common form of mental illness in Italy—especially prevalent among people from the farming areas of the south who were compelled to emigrate to find work. Even if they simply moved to the northern part of Italy, difficulties in adjusting to a colder climate, urban living conditions and unfamiliar cultural pressures put strains on entire families. And the strains were not always relieved

The reaction of a nation is seen in the
face of Chief Petty Officer Graham
Jackson, who weeps as he plays "Goin'
Home" on his accordion while President
Franklin Roosevelt's coffin is carried to
the train in Warm Springs, Georgia, after
his death in April 1945. The national loss
triggered a general state of depression.
Soldiers throughout the world wept;
in front of the White House people stood
transfixed for hours at a time; and
everywhere a sense of shock was felt.

by a return home. Dr. Simone cited the case of a man from the Abruzzo region who left his wife and children to seek work in the United States. For 15 years he toiled as a street cleaner in a large city, living in squalor so he could send funds home and save whatever he could. Finally he returned to his hometown with enough money to buy a house and settle down comfortably. But the way of life he had looked forward to was no longer possible; the town itself had changed. His expectations dashed, he began to brood over the injustice of his lot, sank deeper and deeper into depression and finally tried to kill himself.

The environmental influences that may plunge an individual into depression are not necessarily geographic. The gigantic government under which he lives, the impersonal corporation he works for, his own family —all these can generate what Frederic Flach has called a depressogenic environment. The family environment is perhaps the most potent. The individual may be thwarted in his desire for independence and at the same time may be saddled with anxiety that he cannot survive without the family's emotional support. He may be on the receiving end of subliminal messages—for example, "I love you, in spite of the kind of person you are"—that undermine his self-esteem. Some family members may constantly stir feelings of guilt in him and also misinterpret his motives so that he begins to doubt his own perceptions, even if accurate. Competitiveness that springs from jealousy, restraints upon humor, refusal to permit shows of emotion, the blocking of open, direct communication—all these, Flach noted, are also elements of a depressive environment. Moreover, Flach added, depression can be contagious —infecting spouse, children and siblings—because chronic depression in one family member can be used as a way of expressing anger indirectly against others, making them feel helpless, guilty and confused.

A study of the family role in depression, made in 1954 by Mabel Blake Cohen of the Washington School of Psychiatry, centered on the home situation, personality and relationships of 12 manic-depressives. In all cases, it turned out, the patients came from families that considered themselves socially inferior but were determined to better themselves. Family aspirations centered on one child—the future depressive—who was expected to succeed in a highly competitive career situation. As a result of his background and expectations, the child grew into a highly conforming, hard-working and overconscientious adult. When the depressive episode struck, usually it was triggered by some failure or rejection—either real or imagined—that made the patient believe he had failed his family.

The Cohen study was criticized because of the small number of cases studied, as well as on the ground that there are many underprivileged, upward-striving and competitive families that do not produce manic-depressives. Still, the findings help to buttress the generally accepted view that various influences in an individual's early life can predispose him to depression. He may be influenced to regard himself as bad, unattractive or incapable. Personality traits may be developed that can make him too rigid to deal flexibly with inevitable disappointments and rejections. Henry P. Laughlin, professor of psychiatry at George Washington University, suggested that depression is more likely to affect individuals who are humorless and overconscientious, who repress normal feelings of anger and hostility, and who embrace standards of perfection that permit no compromise with reality.

However important the cause of a depression may be, it does not matter much in the first step of treatment: recognizing that the problem exists. Obvious as that may seem, refusal to acknowledge a depressed state is common. In mild or moderate depressions, the victim —and the people around him—may pass off a serious attack as a temporary siege of the blues. Even when the condition is chronic, one survey has shown, as long as two to five years may elapse before the sufferer will seek professional help.

Sometimes, however, there may be an immediate and dramatic call for help in the form of a suicide attempt. Paradoxically, severely depressed people are too withdrawn to try this way out. It is beyond their capacity physically and emotionally, whereas a moderately depressed person is able to follow through on a sudden impulse. In any case, psychiatrists unanimously agree that one of the most fallacious bits of folklore is that the person who talks about suicide is just talking. The fact is that most suicide attempts are preceded by a warning from the victim—some chance remark such as "I'd be better off dead," or "the family would be better off without me." Fortunately, a growing number of suicidal people make last-minute, desperate pleas for help to antisuicide organizations, such as the Save-A-Life League in the United States and the Samaritans in Britain, which operate 24-hour telephone services credited with saving thousands of lives a year. Trained social workers try to calm the often hysterical caller, then guide him to a hospital or counseling agency that provides assistance and therapy.

When a depression victim seeks a more conventional route out of his difficulties by enlisting a psychiatrist's services, the course of action is twofold. The degree of the depression—mild, moderate or severe—must be determined, and its root cause probed. How long the probing may

During the middle of the day on December 19th, Tromsø's rainswept main street is aglitter with lights and gay Christmas decorations.

A darkness at noon in Norway

In Tromsø, Norway, from November to the latter part of January, the street lights are on around the clock, and houses are ablaze with light except when people are trying to sleep. The bright lights are an attempt to banish the darkness and the gloom that beset the community during that period. In Tromsø, a city of 40,000 lying 200 miles above the Arctic circle, the sun never rises for 58 days in the winter.

The polar blackness, or *morketiden*, as the Norwegians call it, produces a variety of bizarre effects. People who are healthy during the rest of the year become lethargic, edgy, fearful and severely depressed. "During the winter," says psychiatrist Harald Reppesgaard of Asgard Mental Hospital, "the whole city slows down. People's concentration and work capacity are reduced and they are always tired." Though no one can explain why, people have trouble sleeping and children's growth slows as well. Babies cry more, in the Tromsø winter. Sales of cod liver oil, vitamin pills, sedatives, pep pills, sleeping pills—and alcohol—soar.

The people of Tromsø look forward to the reappearance of the sun on January 21—*Soldag*, or sun day—the way that children anticipate Christmas, and when it comes, schools and offices close and there are feasts and celebrations.

take is unpredictable; among other reasons, in many cases of depression the causes are multiple, and need untangling. So-called middle-aged depression is a good example of the complexity. This severe, lingering ailment is categorized as endogenous, and indeed at least two causes to which it is ascribed are internal in origin: one, biological changes brought on by age; the other, deep-seated psychological fears that the best years of life have gone by. Yet external stress situations may also induce this depression—compulsory retirement from a job, for instance, or the departure from home of the last child.

Measuring the depth of a depression has been made easier in recent years with the development of a specific diagnostic tool—a rating scale for depression. A patient's rating is based solely upon his symptoms, either as voiced by him or as observed by a trained psychiatric worker. The objective is first to try to determine if the patient is depressed and, if so, to gauge the depth of the depression.

One widely used rating scale is a depression inventory, developed by Aaron Beck. Beck based his work on the premise that the "key factor in diagnosing depression is *change* in the psychobiological systems" —change, in short, in the patient's physiology, behavior, emotions, motivations and cognition, or view of himself. To measure the changes the inventory poses 21 sets of statements; in each set, the patient is asked to choose the statement most applicable to him at that moment. For example, among the cognitive changes that are looked for is a decline in the patient's estimate of his ability to make decisions. He is presented with four statements:

I make decisions about as well as ever.

I try to put off making decisions.

I have great difficulty in making decisions.

I can't make any decisions at all any more.

Other sets of statements probe such areas as the patient's ability to sleep and work, suicidal thoughts, sexual drive and interest in other people. The more negative the response, the higher the overall score—and the more severe the depression.

The diagnosis of a patient's depressed state—whether by rating scale or by the psychiatrist's own observations—serves as the guideline to choice of treatment. But whether the case is mild, moderate or severe, and whether the cause is known or unknown, most treatments nowadays concentrate on combining psychotherapy and antidepressant drugs.

Two classes of antidepressant medication in widespread use today are the so-called tricyclics and the MAO—for monoamine oxidase—inhibitors. These increase the flow of chemical substances in the brain that are reduced or blocked in depressive states. A third medication, used increasingly in cases of manic depression, is lithium, which affects the levels of sodium, potassium, magnesium and calcium in the body; it appears that if these vital minerals are not present in correct amounts depression may occur. How lithium acts is not yet fully understood. Indeed the entire subject of how drugs alleviate mental disturbances is still under intensive study *(Chapter 5)*.

Once the medication has attacked the biochemical base of the depression, the therapist can begin to explore with the patient the emotional problems that contribute to the ailment. In severe cases, the therapy may initially consist of setting simple tasks for the patient in an attempt to alter the behavior that has become patterned during the illness. For example, the patient tries to rise at a certain hour, make his bed or wash the dishes after each meal. Even by taking such elementary steps, a depression victim may feel that he has a measure of control over his actions and may gradually build confidence until he is able to manage the activities of normal everyday living.

Depression treatment can also be oriented toward the patient's cultural background. In Tokyo, psychiatrist Shōma Morita originated a treatment with roots in the contemplative philosophy of Zen Buddhism. During the first week, the patient is isolated in a hospital room where he lies abed, "facing his sufferings all day." The second week is devoted to light tasks, such as gardening or sweeping, followed the next week by harder physical tasks. The fourth and final week of hospitalization permits the patient some freedom to take a walk or to go shopping. During the treatment, an aide or psychiatrist is constantly at hand—even during the isolation stage—but he says nothing. He does, however, respond —in writing—to remarks written in a diary the patient is required to keep. For example, if a diary entry says "I can't believe I am getting better," the psychiatrist may reply: "When you are not sure, please suffer —don't try to get rid of the suffering."

Throughout, the main aim of the treatment is not to understand the symptoms and origin of the depression according to Western psychoanalytic principles, but to get the patient to accept the fact that he has these depressed feelings—even to welcome them, and adjust to them if they do not dissipate. Such treatment is apparently effective in a traditional Japanese cultural setting, which fosters acceptance of things as they are, but most observers believe it would not work in Western societies that encourage active struggle against difficulties.

With increasing successes in the treatment of depression, the next major thrust in coping with this global problem may be the emergence

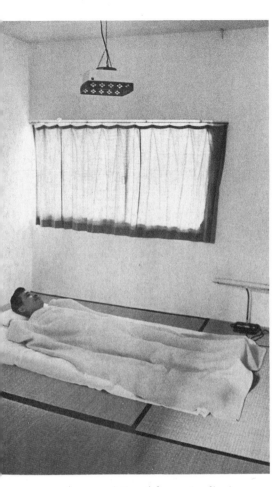

A young victim of depression lies in a partially darkened "isolation hell" as part of Morita therapy, which requires him to do nothing but "face his sufferings." This treatment has had considerable success in the traditional Japanese culture, where people are taught to accept their fates, but most psychiatrists doubt its effectiveness in the West, where people learn aggression rather than submission.

of preventive techniques. Prevention now is primarily a matter of getting to victims earlier so as to arrest the condition, and of fending off relapses through drugs and therapy. But specialists in the field are now thinking in terms of defeating depression even before it has a chance to take hold. New discoveries about genetic factors may someday be used to help identify possible depressives and steer them away from the ailment by special training. Some experts believe that educating people to recognize a depressing environment will help them deal more intelligently with the dilemma such an environment creates for them. An individual may choose to leave the soulless corporation where he is employed and take a job with a smaller firm in which he counts for more. He can make a start at relieving family tensions by insisting on franker communication between the members.

Perhaps most important, he can try to reevaluate his concepts of himself. According to Aaron Beck, every individual has such concepts —"clusters of attitudes about himself"—both favorable and unfavorable. What matters is the value he applies to the unfavorable concept. An individual courts trouble not because he thinks he is weak or unattractive but because he then makes negative generalizations about these traits, such as "I'm no good because I'm weak" or "I'm nothing because I'm unattractive." Such sweeping, negative generalizations should be avoided. An individual can indeed identify and attempt to change realistic defects. Or he can simply—and healthily—accept certain imperfections and learn to live with them as part of his own unique self. As Beck pointed out: "Not all people who regard themselves as physically, mentally, or socially deficient consider these traits bad nor are repelled by them. I have interviewed several intellectually and physically handicapped people who do not attach a negative value to their disabilities and who have never shown any depressive tendencies."

Even for people who experience depression there is hope. Despite the profound suffering it causes, it is unlike many physical illnesses in that recovery is total. Depression does not leave the individual with a weakened heart, for example, or the partial loss of mobility. In fact, depression can help an individual to find a more satisfying and meaningful life. Frederic Flach, in a book entitled *The Secret Strength of Depression,* noted that many people rebound from depression better able to cope, often reaching new levels of creativity. The illness, he wrote, enables a person to examine, then relinquish, old assumptions that block a fresh appraisal of the possibilities in life. "To experience acute depression," Flach concluded, "is an opportunity for a person not just to learn more about himself, but to become more whole than he was."

The gloom of the uprooted

Psychologists say that loneliness, alienation, and feelings of social inadequacy and inferiority are among the commonest causes of reactive depression—the kind that occurs in response to a particular environment or situation. Few groups experience these feelings more acutely than do immigrant workers. Transported from their native lands to unfamiliar and often hostile environments, they are subject to homesickness and prejudice, and separated from the mainstream of their new life by the strangeness of the people, language and customs. Considering the array of serious problems that they face, it is no surprise that immigrant workers have one of the highest incidences of depression to be found among any group of people in the world.

In recent years, after a boom in Germany's economy created a labor shortage, large numbers of immigrants arrived to work in the country: Turks, Portuguese, Spaniards, Yugoslavs and Italians—2.6 million in all. The Germans call these immigrants *Gastarbeiter,* or guest workers. But the workers themselves do not feel very much like guests; the *Gastarbeiter* finds himself cut off from his loved ones, looked down upon by the people around him, sexually frustrated and unable to sustain his self-esteem.

Some 600,000 of Germany's foreign workers come from Turkey, and their plight has been studied by Rana Kartal, a Turkish psychiatrist. During the average three- to five-year stay in Germany, 90 per cent of his countrymen, says Kartal, will develop some of the signs of depression, ranging in severity from headaches to incapacitating periods of gloom.

Winding up a two-day train ride, weary Turkish workers arrive at the Munich station at 5 a.m. and head for a room in the basement to wait for job assignments. Overwhelmed by their first glimpse of a highly industrialized city, they are already feeling alienated and anxious.

PHOTOGRAPHED BY GILLES PERESS

Listless and bored, newly arrived Turks wait at a dispatch center for work assignments.

Doing the work no one else will do

The Turkish immigrants are brought in primarily to do unskilled work—as garbage men, street laborers and assembly-line workers. Though these jobs are no more menial than the farming they did in Turkey, the workers soon learn that most Germans shun such employment. Consequently, psychiatrist Rana Kartal points out, the Turks suffer loss of self-esteem and when—as is usually the case —they cannot get better jobs, their self-doubt may develop into a depressing sense of inadequacy.

As unheeding Munich pedestrians hasten by, a Turkish street cleaner wields his broom in a plaza. Some 65 per cent of Munich's street cleaners are foreign.

Turkish workers housed in the barracks
of a factory 20 miles outside of Munich
spend Sunday at what for them is a
humiliating and unmanly task: washing
their clothes and hanging them up to dry.

The quarters of this converted trailer set
up at a building site are cramped even
when only three of the four construction
workers who live in it are present. But
when Turks try to move out of company
housing, they often encounter prejudice.

Demeaned by an alien life style

A 1963 study by two Italian psychologists of mental illness among immigrant workers in Milan showed that the change in their life styles was a major factor in causing depression, ranking second only to monotony on the job.

The experience of the Turkish workers in Germany bears out this finding. Most of them have been used to living close to nature in widely scattered huts in their homeland, and they find their regimented, barracks-style existence in Germany demeaning. In addition, they feel their manhood threatened by the necessity to perform chores that, back home in their native Turkey, were attended to strictly by women.

Unable to eat German food, which may contain pork and other ingredients their Muslim religion forbids, dejected Turkish workers at a dormitory in Munich must spend their free time at the unfamiliar task of preparing meals.

The struggle to fill the empty hours

"When he comes to Germany," says Kartal, "the Turkish worker experiences a total cutoff from his loved ones. If he is among the 20 per cent who are illiterate, he cannot even write those at home except through a stranger. The sense of isolation brought on by these circumstances can be devastating."

The attempts of the workers to combat their loneliness meet with only limited success. The language barrier, local girls' distaste for their "foreign" appearance and manners, and lack of money keep them apart from the community. Says an ex-worker: "There is endless entertainment in Germany, but we couldn't afford it. Finally, our greatest pleasure was listening to The Voice of Turkey on the radio."

Trying to catch a Munich girl's eye, two Turks receive only an averted gaze in response. Because 70 per cent of the men must live without women while in Germany, lack of sexual satisfaction is their most important single frustration.

Dressed in their best, Turks from miles around congregate on Sunday morning in Munich's train station, where they will spend most of the day at the stand-up snack counters, exchanging news and reminiscences about life at home.

On Saturday night, dateless and homesick workers flock to a Munich nightclub where they can hear Turkish songs that recall faraway villages and mosques, or that express the yearning for unattainable feminine companionship.

Spruced up and clutching a bunch of roses, Gastarbeiter on their day off pose in Berlin for pictures to be sent back to Turkey. Anxious to conceal the strain of their empty lives, the workers regularly send such photos to their families as evidence they are thriving.

Turkish workers seeking solace for their problems pray in a recently built Munich mosque. "It is customary," says Kartal, "for Turks to consult the imam [Muslim priest] even before a doctor when they are ill. This tendency undoubtedly has some bearing on the large number of Gastarbeiter who turn to their religion during their time in Germany."

Succumbing to overwhelming feelings of despair, a Turkish street cleaner in Munich buries his face in his hands. He is taking a 6 a.m. coffee break after two hours working at his solitary, menial job in the dark, silent streets of the sleeping city. At such moments, despite his bravest efforts, the accumulated woes of a Gastarbeiter can make him despondent. But the men are resilient. Once they return to their native villages, their depression usually disappears.

The Mind Imprisoned

4

Psychosis is the mental disturbance that the average person finds most mysterious and most frightening—understandably, for it is a serious illness. Thinking, mood and behavior are so grossly distorted that victims typically cannot meet the demands of everyday life. There is always a serious break with reality: the psychotic cannot see the world as it is or think about it in logical ways. His emotional reactions are inappropriate or extravagant, and his actions are bizarre and often primitive, as the following dialogue between a patient and psychiatrist suggests:

Psychiatrist: Well, you seem pretty happy today.

Mental patient: Happy! Happy! You certainly are a master of understatement, you rogue! Why, I'm ecstatic. I'm leaving for the West Coast today, on my daughter's bicycle. Only 3,100 miles. That's nothing, you know. I could probably walk, but I want to get there by next week. And along the way I plan to follow up on my inventions of the past month, you know, stopping at the big plants along the way having lunch with the executives, maybe getting to know them a bit—you know, Doc, "know" in the Biblical sense. Oh God, how good it feels.

Such an unfortunate exists in a realm of his own, alive, yet to family and friends lost almost as if dead. Psychosis is tragically common—according to one estimate, 15 million people around the world fall victim to psychosis at one time or another during their lives. Its impact is heightened because one of the most common disabling forms, schizophrenia, is frequently seen among young adults; more people 25 to 34 years old than those of any other age group are stricken so severely they must be hospitalized. Many of them, of course, are parents of young children, and the blow to their families is severe. Children are not as likely to be stricken as adults, but the presence of one psychotic child can have a devastating effect on the lives of everyone else in the family.

Despite the relatively high incidence of psychosis, however, the outlook for psychotics—and for their families—is far from bleak; indeed, it has brightened considerably in recent years. Psychotic episodes are frequently brought on by reactions to acute situations, and may disappear when the situation itself changes; furthermore, some psychotics will improve with time regardless of whether they are treated or not. More important than either of these ameliorating factors are new drugs and therapeutic techniques, which are restoring a majority of psychotic patients to reasonably normal lives. Very rarely does a breakdown today condemn someone to a lifetime in an institutional cell. During the first quarter of this century, 60 per cent of schizophrenics were expected to be hospitalized for the rest of their lives. In 1962, a study in Britain showed that of patients sent to hospitals five years earlier, only 11 per cent were still there. All over the world, hospital populations have declined *(page 139)* as psychotics have been released; if not all have been cured, at least they have been able to function. And new understanding of possible physical causes of psychosis promises further progress against these illnesses.

Psychosis is not one illness but many and the symptoms are often bewildering, even to experts. Many of its characteristics can be seen in neurosis too. The difference is a matter of degree to many authorities. According to the "unitary" theory of mental disturbance, all psychological disorders are at bottom one: qualitatively alike and only quantitatively different. The neurotic's view of reality is somewhat askew in some respects; the psychotic's conception is flagrantly distorted in most respects.

The unitary view is quite generally applied to one mental disturbance, depression *(Chapter 3)*, which has both neurotic and psychotic forms. There are ailments, on the other hand, that are held by many authorities to be distinctively psychotic. They believe that there are qualitative as well as quantitative distinctions between neurosis and psychosis. One difference lies in awareness. Usually the neurotic knows that something is the matter with him; the psychotic is ordinarily oblivious to his condition. A related distinction is the patient's tolerance for his disturbance. The neurotic generally wants to be rid of his neurosis; the psychotic is likely to accept his derangement. As psychoanalyst Silvano Arieti explained it, the psychotic "does not fight his disorder, as does the psychoneurotic, but lives in it."

Psychoses can be divided into two categories. One is the functional, in which psychological factors are believed to play a major role though there may be biological causes too. The other is the organic type, caused by fairly readily identifiable brain damage. Organic psychosis can result if the brain is intoxicated by alcohol, LSD, lead, mercury or certain poisonous gases. It may be damaged by vitamin deficiencies or a defect

George III of Britain, who ruled during the American Revolution, was dubbed the Mad King. He suffered from delusions and hallucinations and was subject to rages so uncontrollable he had to be confined in a strait jacket. In 1969 a study by two English psychiatrists revealed that his psychosis was physical in origin, stemming from a hereditary disease of the nervous system called porphyria.

in the body's use of food. The brain may be infected by syphilis or malaria, or impaired by arteriosclerosis or a tumor.

The effects of organic psychosis can be shocking, as the case of Charles Whitman illustrates. In 1966, while a student at the University of Texas, Whitman wrote a grimly irrational note: "I intend to kill my wife after I pick her up from work. I love her very much." That evening he killed his mother and stabbed his wife. The next morning, carrying three rifles, a shotgun and two pistols, he climbed to the observation deck of a 307-foot tower at the university, and killed 14 people and wounded 31 others on the campus below before being gunned down by the police. Whitman had been complaining of headaches for a long time and an autopsy disclosed a malignant tumor in his brain. Such cases, fortunately, are rare.

Among the functional psychoses, the most common and most serious are a number of ailments loosely grouped as the schizophrenias. This syndrome afflicted the dancer Vaslav Nijinsky, the playwright August Strindberg and the novelist Scott Fitzgerald's celebrated wife Zelda.

Worldwide, about 1 per cent of the population is thought to be schizophrenic. Psychiatrist Stanley F. Yolles and biostatistician Morton Kramer have estimated that about 3 per cent of all American males who live to be at least 15 years old will show signs of schizophrenia before they die. It afflicts more men than women—no one knows why. In Europe, the comparable figure is given as 1 per cent, probably because European psychiatrists diagnose it less often than American doctors do, using a variety of other labels for syndromes that would be called schizophrenia in the United States. No culture is exempt, but some peoples in communal societies—including the Chinese and the Eskimos—are more tolerant than Westerners of schizophrenic behavior and less likely to consider its victims sick.

The reason for differences in diagnosis is that schizophrenia is not a clear-cut disorder like tuberculosis or diabetes. Seymour Kety, a leading authority, commented, "Schizophrenia is not a disease, it's an opinion." Although the experts cannot reconcile their diverse opinions, most do agree on certain common symptoms: social and emotional withdrawal, distorted thinking and bizarre language and behavior. They also agree that the schizophrenic's whole personality is disorganized and that every aspect of his functioning is affected.

The schizophrenic crawls into his shell both socially and emotionally. He withdraws his interest and attention from people and events and retreats into a private inner sphere. Usually he suffers from emotional "blunting": nothing in external reality gives him pleasure, and he may be apathetic even about the outbreak of war or the death of a parent. His realm of fantasy is often less a sanctuary than a dungeon. One of R. D. Laing's patients thought of it as a cave and wrote this poem:

There is no gentleness, no softness, no warmth in this deep cave.
My hands have felt along the cave's stony sides, and, in every crevice,
    there is only black depth.
Sometimes, there is almost no air . . .
There is no opening, no outlet,
I am imprisoned.

The schizophrenic's confused thinking shows up most strikingly in hallucinations and delusions. Hallucinations (seeing or hearing or feeling something not there) and delusions (believing in implausible ideas) often occur together. One hospitalized mental patient thought a former boy friend—by then dead—was still pursuing her, and she could see and hear him and feel his touch when he came to visit her. Every night she approached the attendant on her ward, demanding, "Nurse, make Harry get out of my bed."

That patient's false perceptions were mundane compared with the phantasmagoric and cataclysmic visions of some schizophrenics. Anton Boisen, who emerged from schizophrenia to become a hospital chaplain, wrote in a memoir: "It seemed that a lot of new worlds were forming. There was music everywhere and rhythm and beauty. I heard what seemed to be a choir of angels. The next night I was visited, not by angels, but by a lot of witches. From the ventilator shaft I picked up paper black cats and broom-sticks and poke bonnets. I finally not only worked out a way of checking the invasion of the black cats, but I found some sort of process of regeneration which could be used to save other people." Eventually, wrote Boisen, "I found that by lying flat on the floor near the ventilator shaft, I could hear the most beautiful voice I had ever heard. It was the celebration of the Last Supper."

During the time the schizophrenic is caught up in his psychosis, his language is nearly always cryptic. What he says may be so disjointed that it has been called a word salad. At times his speech is enlivened with words he coins, many of them quite appropriate and imaginative. One patient called his ward psychiatrist a "temperatrist" to suggest the doctor tempered justice with mercy. Schizophrenic sentences are often built of words associated in meaning or sound. "I may be a blue baby but social baby not, but yet a blue heart baby could be in the blue book published just before the war," one patient wrote. Another set down these words: "Are you pure? Sure? Yes! Yes! Yes! Frame! Name! Same! Same! Same! Came." Often a schizophrenic utterance sounds portentous but is hard to fathom. One psychotic seems to have intended something important when he wrote, "The subterfuge and the mistaken planned substitutions for that demanded American action can produce nothing but the general results of negative contention."

The schizophrenic's behavior is as odd as his language. One patient, Lara Jefferson, drew word portraits of her fellows and nicknamed them according to their characteristic actions. There was Claw-belly, who kept her abdomen "scratched and clawed and over-turned in great red welts and ridges." But, Jefferson wrote, "I like 'Claw-belly'—for she rose up and danced on the day I was put into a jacket. She danced to my singing —a wild, whirling dance—and she was stark naked." The Medicine-maker "was sitting out in the day hall with a heavy over-hanging black forelock brought down from her forehead and tied with a strip of bath-toweling. She sprang out before me, then flung her arms wide and bowed low," wrote Jefferson. "What she said to me seemed very convincing: 'Welcome, stranger—welcome among us. But remember, remember always that I am the great Medicine-maker of this tribe.'" As for the Dancer, "they found her standing at one of the windows on the ward up-stairs, broadcasting a radio message to the President through a hand mir-ror." The beautiful, graceful Pagan also stood at a window, "howling at the morning." Jefferson was certain that Dante could have "heard nothing in hell more blood-curdling."

Schizophrenia occurs in several forms, each so different from the others that experts used to consider them distinct psychoses. Each shows the general characteristics of schizophrenia—withdrawal, confused thinking, and odd speech and behavior—but the pattern of specific symptoms varies from one form to another. Five of the most important varieties recognized by the American Psychiatric Association are the simple, hebephrenic, catatonic, paranoid and childhood types.

Simple schizophrenia, according to the APA manual, is "less dra-matically psychotic" than most other subvarieties. The victim often is not hospitalized and may pass almost unnoticed. He may hold an un-skilled job needing little contact with others—as a dishwasher, say—but he rarely works long in one place. Many ambulatory schizophrenics live alone in rooming houses, watching TV all day or wandering the streets. Others are derelicts, sleeping in doorways or flophouses and car-rying their worldly goods in shopping bags. Wherever they live, simple schizophrenics lead sharply restricted lives. They seldom have friends and do not care: indeed, apathy is their most notable characteristic.

In hebephrenic schizophrenia, personality disintegration is especial-ly severe. The patient ignores even the rudiments of personal care: he

Healing the child to save the adult

"He'll grow out of it" are the placating words that many parents hear when a clinic turns away disturbed toddlers. Though psychiatric treatment of the very young is generally believed unwarranted, Dr. Eleanor Galenson, director of New York's Therapeutic Nursery of the Albert Einstein College of Medicine, believes serious symptoms—semimute withdrawal, continuing violent rages —should be treated, even in tots.

The college nursery focuses on each child all the attention of his mother and a therapist. With much loving, listening and urging, they lead the child to accept himself—many cannot bear to look in a mirror *(opposite)*. As the child gains self-confidence, he establishes relationships that will help him grow up to enjoy a normally active life.

A therapist engages the gaze of a troubled child to draw her attention outside herself.

Three therapists try to involve their charges in drawing to express emotions. Only one child (left) complies. The little boy at center can bring himself to watch, but the third child (right) always darts to and from the table.

Playing with blocks in her role as a therapist at the nursery, a mother encourages her four-year-old son —who previously would do nothing but work puzzles all by himself—to engage in activities with another person.

Encouraged by the therapist at her right, a disturbed girl attempts to scrawl an image of herself over her reflection in a mirror—a first step in identifying the reflection as her own and establishing herself as an independent individual.

rarely bathes, his clothing is in disarray and his toilet habits become infantile. Frequently he makes strange gestures, talks baby talk, has tantrums and giggles inappropriately. The psychiatrist Silvano Arieti described a hebephrenic woman of 30 who "lay on the floor in the corridor, turned the radio loud, jumped and stamped, shouted at her psychiatrist from the far end of the ward. When milk was spilled on the table, she licked it."

The third major type of schizophrenia, catatonia, is marked by immobility broken by uncontrollable excitement. The patient stays motionless for hours, usually in an uncomfortable posture, perhaps with an arm extended or a leg held off the floor. One catatonic girl would go to a corner of her ward every morning, pull the neck of her dress over her head, and stand there all day except when an attendant propelled her to the dining room. Another patient, on the way to recovery, said he had believed he would die if he moved even an eye muscle. Most catatonics are negativistic. They resist doing what people want them to do or deliberately do the opposite. When they are prodded too much—or with no apparent provocation—their rigid torpor can explode. Then they strike out violently at the nearest person or turn their fury on themselves. One patient gouged his own eye before he could be restrained.

The paranoid schizophrenic is distinguished by delusions of persecution and grandeur. The stereotype of the psychotic, the patient who thinks he is Napoleon, suffers from this ailment. Vivid hallucinations may buttress his delusions. Voices threaten him, shimmering lights assure him God is on his side, electrical rays from his enemies' arsenal pierce him. One patient, still in the throes of his psychosis, wrote: "I was once more startled by those same pursuers. As before, I could catch part of their talk but, in the theatre crowds, I could see them nowhere. I heard one of them, a woman, say: 'You can't get away from us; we'll lay for you, and get you after a while!' Believe-it-or-not, some of them, besides being able to tell a person's thoughts, are also able to project their magnetic voices—commonly called 'radio voices' around here—a distance of a few miles without talking loud, and without apparent effort, their voices sounding from that distance as tho heard thru a radio head-set, this being done without electrical apparatus."

One notorious victim of paranoid schizophrenia was Robert Kennedy's assassin, Sirhan Sirhan. Sirhan's disordered mind blamed Kennedy for the terror he had experienced as a boy when Palestinians and Zionists fought in Jerusalem; he came to believe it his patriotic duty to kill Kennedy. As this case shows, the paranoid's personality does not necessarily fall apart completely. But his personal relationships

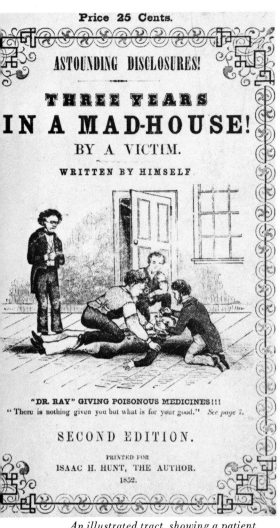

Price 25 Cents.

ASTOUNDING DISCLOSURES!

THREE YEARS
IN A MAD-HOUSE!
BY A VICTIM.

WRITTEN BY HIMSELF

"DR. RAY" GIVING POISONOUS MEDICINES!!!
"There is nothing given you but what is for your good." *See page 7.*

SECOND EDITION.

PRINTED FOR
ISAAC H. HUNT, THE AUTHOR.
1852.

An illustrated tract, showing a patient being force-fed a "poisonous medicine," depicts one of the horrors of mental hospitals in the U.S. in the 1850s. Part of a campaign to improve the wretched conditions in mental institutions, such exposés helped to bring about legislation improving mental patients' care and treatment, and protecting their rights.

are stormy because he suspects relative, friend and stranger alike.

Perhaps the most tragic victims of schizophrenia are children. One childhood ailment that many authorities have long considered a form of schizophrenia—though others now disagree—is particularly severe, though fortunately rare: infantile autism. The chief symptom, an extraordinary aloneness, usually appears in the first year of life. Autistic babies rarely look at anyone. They do not reach out, as normal infants do, when they are about to be picked up; when they are held, they keep their bodies completely rigid. While ignoring people, autistic children are fascinated by objects and can become greatly attached to a flashlight or camera. Sameness obsesses them; when objects they have ritualistically arranged are moved, or their routines are changed, they often explode in fearful tantrums, which may last for hours. They can be both destructive and self-destructive: some of them continually bang their heads against walls and must wear tiny helmets for protection.

Many autistic children are mute. Even those who speak have minimal vocabularies and often repeat words and phrases meaninglessly. Indicative of the autistic child's inability to relate to himself or to others is a failure to use personal pronouns, especially "I." Bruno Bettelheim, the Austrian-born American psychoanalyst widely known for his work with children, describes the responses of Marcia, an autistic girl of 11, to the question, "Do you want to go out?" If she did want to, she would at first reply, "Want go out." Later she said, "You want go out." Martha, another autistic girl, said "You hid your face" to describe her own behavior, and to tell what she did on a shopping expedition, she said, "She touched the toys in Wolf's toy store. Martha did it, and Wolf did not like it."

Many people erroneously assume that an autistic child is mentally retarded; he may be very intelligent. Some autistic youngsters memorize long lists of names after only one or two hearings. Asked questions, they may give answers that at first sound irrelevant but on reflection prove appropriate. When Donald, an autistic boy, was asked to subtract four from 10, he replied, "I'll draw a hexagon"—a six-sided figure. Given a typewriter, a mute autistic child who has never been taught to read or write may type his own name or parts of commercials.

People who act in such strange ways obviously have something wrong with their thought processes. Since little is known about how humans think, the causes of functional psychosis remain elusive. The aberrant behavior could be entirely learned, a consequence of environment. Or it could result from malfunctioning in certain brain circuits, a defect that might be at least partially inherited. Statistical studies of schizo-

phrenia among identical twins—who share identical inherited traits —strongly suggest that heredity is involved. But psychoses do not simply and inevitably run in families. Most psychiatrists now believe both heredity and environment play a role. The genes, it appears, may make an individual vulnerable to schizophrenia, but the disorder will probably not develop unless it is triggered by stress in the environment. However, the evidence is not all in yet, and there is still controversy over the relative importance of nature and nurture.

Separating the influences of heredity and environment has proved very difficult. Surveys of schizophrenia have found that the parents and children of schizophrenics are about 10 times more likely to have the disorder than people in the general population. But these studies prove nothing about inheritance, since family environment, regardless of genetics, is a crucial determinant of behavior. Even studies of twins raised from birth in different environments cannot escape all the pitfalls of this complex research. Such respected investigators as David Rosenthal and Seymour Kety believe that "with practically no exception," twin studies "did not scrupulously avoid . . . subjective bias." If a researcher believes either that schizophrenia is a genetic disorder or that it is environmentally caused, he may make mistakes that will influence his findings. Errors can be made in terming a set of twins identical rather than fraternal. Also, the diagnosis of schizophrenia is subjective; a person so labeled by one clinician might be differently diagnosed by another. And when a diagnostician knows he is studying the twin of a schizophrenic, that knowledge may influence his diagnosis.

Rosenthal, Kety and their colleagues believe they have found ways both of separating genetic and environmental influences and of eliminating the effect of bias. Their studies, made principally in Denmark, avoid the use of twins but do depend on comparisons between people who had been adopted and others raised by their natural parents.

In one of their investigations, 33 schizophrenics adopted in early childhood were compared to a control group of 33 adopted individuals with no history of mental illness. A search was made for all parents and siblings—adopted or related by blood—of the 66 cases, but the researchers were not told whether they were looking for relatives of subjects or of controls. Then four diagnosticians studied health data compiled on the relatives. They also worked "blind": the material was coded so they could not know if they were studying subject or control relatives, or if the relationship was biological or adoptive. The decoded findings showed schizophrenia-like disturbances in 13 biological relatives of subjects, but only three such cases in biological relatives of controls. No such difference in the incidence of schizophrenia was found among adoptive relatives of either subjects or controls.

Although scientists are a long way from finding a specific "bad gene" that causes schizophrenia, they are convinced, Kety says, that "schizophrenia is genetically influenced." They are equally certain that it is environmentally influenced too, because in about half the sets of identical twins studied for schizophrenia one twin remains well. Family environment seems to be the decisive factor.

Among those who have investigated the role of the family is Theodore Lidz. He and his colleagues at the Yale Psychiatric Institute made a long-term study of the families of 16 hospitalized schizophrenics. The researchers interviewed every family member again and again, several of them hundreds of times, in an effort "to recreate the personalities, their interactions, the ways and the atmosphere of the family group."

Among their conclusions: "Not a single family was reasonably well integrated. . . . The majority were torn by schismatic conflict between the parents that divided the family into two hostile factions, with each spouse seeking to gain the upper hand, defying the wishes of the other, undercutting the worth of the spouse to the children, seeking to win the children to his side and to use them as emotional replacements for the spouse. The remaining families developed a skewed pattern because the serious psychopathology of the dominant parent was passively accepted by the other, leading to aberrant ways of living and of child-rearing." One of the most pernicious influences, Lidz reported, was that the parents did not resolve their differences but hid them, not only from outsiders but also from themselves. "Their acceptance and masking of the serious problems that existed created a strange emotional environment that was perplexing to the child," Lidz said.

A crucial aspect of this crippling family atmosphere is what anthropologist Gregory Bateson called the double-bind phenomenon. The mother repeatedly conveys a conflicting double message to a child that makes him confused and anxious, and unable to respond. Don Jackson, a colleague of Bateson's, explained, "It's a sort of game, or gambit, set up by the mother so that the child is damned if he does and damned if he doesn't." Bateson wrote of a mother's visit to her schizophrenic son in the hospital: "He was glad to see her and impulsively put his arm around her shoulders, whereupon she stiffened. He withdrew his arm and she asked, 'Don't you love me any more?' He then blushed, and she said, 'Dear, you must not be so easily embarrassed and afraid of your feelings.'" Verbally, the mother urged her son to show affection; nonverbally, by stiffening, she told him to keep away. The dilemma she created for the boy stirred up so much anxiety and anger he ended the visit and, after his mother left, assaulted a hospital aide.

A major criticism of the studies by Lidz, Bateson and others who believe the family environment to be the crucial factor in causing schizophrenia is that the crippling pattern might be a consequence, rather than the cause, of having a schizophrenic in the home. All families interviewed by Lidz and Bateson were already burdened by the presence of a disturbed child, making it possible that the distorted family atmosphere resulted from the schizophrenia and did not cause it.

In either case, a child reared in a distorted environment may withdraw because that is the only way he can survive. As long as possible he presents a front of normality, but behind it, according to Karl Menninger, conflict, resentment and anxiety fester. Under new stresses, Menninger believes, control may become impossible, "the facade may break down and the underlying bitterness and conflict may break through" as symptoms of schizophrenia. Although apparently meaningless, they defend the victim against his conflict. Often the defensive meaning is transparent. In the following conversation reported by Arieti the patient's replies obviously keep him from having to focus on disturbing topics:

Doctor: You seem to want to avoid all possible pain.

Patient: I remember reading about Thomas Paine in a history course.

Doctor: You seem to fear that if you develop any close friends, they will desert you.

Patient: I wonder what's for dessert today.

A schizophrenic's delusions and hallucinations are also defenses against conflicts arising in his surroundings. Freud's contemporary Bleuler described a patient who literally believed he was Switzerland. The idea was bizarre, but investigation showed that the patient felt trapped and in his disordered mind defended himself by choosing to be a free country. A man's paranoid delusion that his wife is poisoning his food may protect him from recognizing that her personality and behavior are poisoning his life.

Recognition of the importance of environment, particularly childhood environment, is a development of this century, and it has exerted a powerful influence on therapy for psychosis, as well as indicating ways to prevent such disturbances. The treatment of psychosis has always depended on its presumed cause. In ancient times, people thought mental illness resulted from possession by demons or represented punishment for sin. It was common practice to banish psychotics, leaving them to die of accidents or starvation, or to survive as "wild men." Many societies resorted to outright torture, frightening psychotics with snakes, depriving them of food and water, beating them, or binding them between mattresses so they suffocated and sometimes died.

Even when the psychotic was regarded as the innocent victim of an incurable affliction, he was likely to be confined—and neglected—in a relative's attic, a jail or an institution worse than a jail. Bedlam, founded in London in 1247, is the most notorious place where mentally disturbed people were chained, beaten, starved and exhibited as objects of amusement, but similar institutions existed elsewhere. In the late 1700s, Philippe Pinel, a French physician, and William Tuke, an English Quaker tea merchant, launched effective reforms in their countries; similar work was begun later in the United States by Dorothea Dix, a New England schoolteacher. All aroused public support for clean, sympathetically operated hospitals that would provide medical therapy and not just custodial care. They established the pattern of institutional treatment that has until recently been common in the West.

Hospitalization remains necessary for some psychotics, to keep them from hurting themselves or others, to provide care not obtainable at home or to offer treatments not practical in clinics. But it has serious drawbacks. Many authorities believe that some psychotics are kept in institutions unnecessarily, partly to get them out of the way so their behavior will not bother the rest of society. These critics of institutions note that confinement itself has ill effects. Mental patients kept from contact with healthy people generally get worse. Even the most stable person feels his balance shaken if he must live without respite among psychotics; he is likely to lose his grip on reality altogether if locked up alone for a prolonged period. These disadvantages of confinement are aggravated by the fact that many mental hospitals provide custodial care rather than treatment; governments often fail to provide funds sufficient for therapy, and institutions officially labeled hospitals may degenerate into chaos. The deficiencies in institutional treatment have led to emphasis on methods that permit most patients to live with their families or in small groups in normal communities.

Modern treatments of psychoses aim mainly at the physical basis of the ailment—though the exact cause remains unknown. Drastic methods, such as destruction of parts of the brain to restrain anxiety and violence, have been largely abandoned; the same results are achieved with techniques that do not affect personality, as surgery often did. Physical treatments now rely mostly on drugs and electroconvulsive therapy (ECT), also called electroshock or shock treatment.

continued on page 119

Raun Kaufman plays alone on a couch, fingering a nest of cups, while seeming to concentrate his attention on some distant object. Autistic children generally show great interest in inanimate objects, but they take little notice of people.

The solitary world of autism

When winsome Raun Kaufman was a little over a year old, his parents made a heartbreaking discovery: he showed symptoms of autism, a form of psychosis in which a child is totally absorbed in himself—according to one theory, because he cannot make sense out of his perceptions. Raun was not deaf, but paid no heed when spoken to; he was not blind, but looked "through" people, never at them. He picked up plastic plates and spun them endlessly; he rocked back and forth and stared into space. Psychiatric tests when he was 20 months old showed him to have a mental level of eight months.

But help was hard to come by; doctors have conflicting views about this baffling childhood disorder, and few institutions attempt therapy for infants. So Raun's parents made a thorough study of autism, and applied professional techniques in a new and loving way to create an intensive program that might break into Raun's own particular world. They plied him with educational toys and bombarded him with stimulation to help him make connections out of his jumbled perceptions.

At first Raun ignored them; then he began to show some annoyance; and later he smiled. By the eighth week of the program he was paying attention when his name was called. By the time he was two he was functioning at his own level or better.

Doctors are wary of drawing broad conclusions from Raun's experience. They still have no sure cure for autism. All they can safely say of the program devised for Raun is that it worked with surprising effectiveness for him.

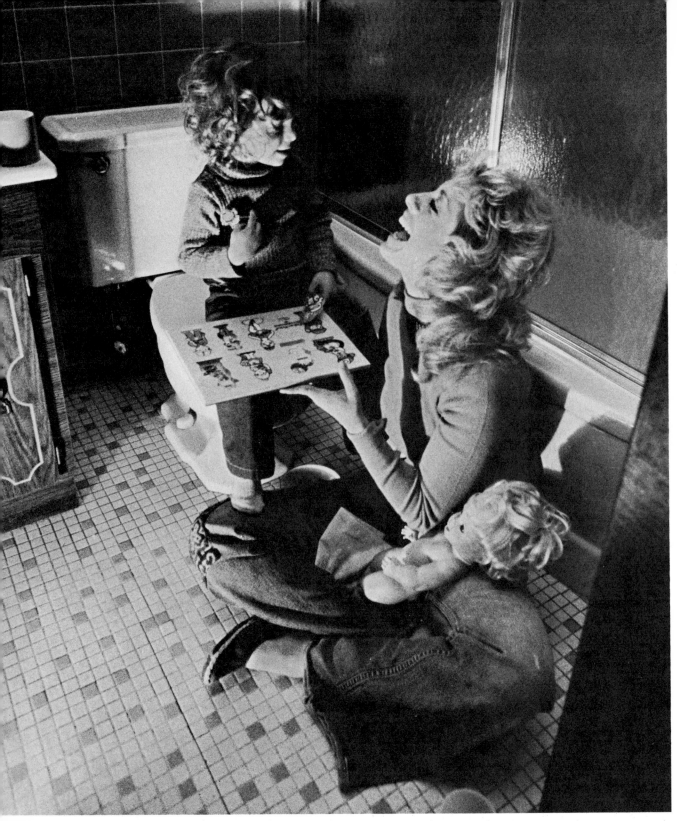

*Raun wins enthusiastic encouragement
from his mother as he works out a puzzle
designed to help him coordinate his
eyes and his hands. His classroom is the
bathroom—an area that was chosen
for its quiet and its lack of distractions.*

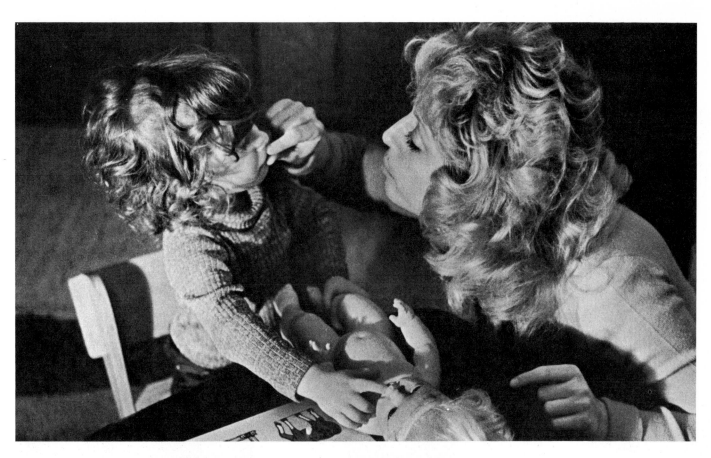

Painstakingly teaching Raun to speak, his
mother touches his mouth while saying
the word herself. Autistic children often
touch, taste and smell inanimate objects,
but seem oblivious to most sights and
sounds. Raun shows he has made a
connection: his small fingers are reaching
out to the mouth of a doll nearby.

Raun's mother and his sisters, Bryn
and Thea, join him in rocking on the floor.
Rhythmic and repetitious motion
fascinates the solitary autistic child. Such
participation in Raun's activities
was made a major part of his therapy.

*Raun gently caresses his father's cheeks,
and meets him eye to eye. Formerly
self-absorbed and heedless of people
around him, Raun learned how to express
interest and proffer affection freely.*

ECT was first used in 1938 by two Italian psychiatrists, Ugo Cerletti and Lucio Bini, after they had observed that epileptic convulsions produced by the drug Metrazol were helpful in treating schizophrenia. The drug proved too risky to use, but the two physicians theorized that electroshock could be controlled and could achieve the same beneficial effects. Their theory proved to be correct.

The procedure is fairly simple. The patient is injected with muscle relaxant and restrained on a bed so he will not hurt himself during the sharp movements induced by the shock. Then some 300 milliamperes of current are sent through his brain to produce a convulsion much like a *grand mal* epileptic seizure. After 10 to 30 minutes of unconsciousness, the patient comes to, but is semistuporous and confused for an hour or two. The principal side effect of ECT is a partial memory loss (generally of events, not of essential learning); it may be temporary or permanent, but it is rarely severe. The treatments cause no pain, yet often terrify patients, many of whom already believe they are being persecuted by malicious doctors using bizarre apparatus. Some psychoanalytically oriented professionals charge terror is the only thing that makes ECT work and consider it barbaric for that reason.

"To shock mental patients . . . finds supporters in every age," Bruno Bettelheim wrote. "This is so, first . . . because it produces results. While stripping the patients of whatever humanity they still have, it makes them, whether out of fear or an intensity of pain, much more pliable. Here it matters little whether this is done, as in past ages, by dunking or whipping or chaining them, or in a more technological age, through medical procedures like lobotomy or electrical shock. Secondly, but not often recognized, it satisfies a desire to punish these recalcitrant objects: because to view them as persons would preclude any use of such procedures."

Whatever the merits of Bettelheim's analysis, ECT remains in use because, as he says, it does work. It is so effective that the drawbacks are accepted by most people. A patient may be totally withdrawn, so drowned in his fantasies that he cannot speak or act, and after two or three treatments walk out not cured, but rational, relaxed, responsive and ready for a normal routine. Others may require more treatments. ECT is a specific for severe depression (and a standard procedure to forestall suicide); after two to 50 treatments, 90 per cent of depressed patients are said to recover, but as many as 50 per cent suffer relapses. As a general treatment in schizophrenia ECT is somewhat less useful: improvement is recorded in two thirds of those treated.

While electroconvulsive therapy remains an essential part of the psychiatrist's armamentarium, its use has declined with the development, since World War II, of a host of "psychoactive" drugs. Tranquilizers, such as the phenothiazines and butyrophenones, calm violent and hyperactive patients, while energizers such as amphetamine arouse withdrawn patients. A third class of drugs, the antidepressants, elevate low moods without causing overexcitement. Chlorpromazine is one of many tranquilizers used to control symptoms of schizophrenia and anxiety states in general. The drugs apparently restore normal brain function so psychotics become rational. New understanding of the way they work *(Chapter 5)* offers clues to the biological causes of psychoses.

Besides such physical treatments as drugs and ECT, some form of psychotherapy is usually provided for psychotics. Freudian psychoanalysis seldom works very well—it is too lengthy and costly to be used widely, and it depends on verbal communication with the patient, which is often impossible. For some illnesses that are resistant to physical treatment—principally childhood schizophrenia and autism—behavior modification techniques are fast gaining ground, although psychotherapy based on psychoanalysis has been traditionally relied on.

One of the most successful psychotherapists is Bettelheim, a Vienna-born psychoanalyst and disciple of Freud. Bettelheim served for a long time as director of the Sonia Shankman Orthogenic School at the University of Chicago. The students there are youngsters so severely disturbed that they have usually been branded untreatable. After two to 10 or more years at the school, 40 per cent of the autistic children and 80 per cent of the others have been rehabilitated.

One key to Bettelheim's success seems to be the school's "total therapeutic milieu," in which even the smallest detail is geared to helping the children. Staff members, from academic teachers and "counselors" to maids and handymen, are chosen for their capacity to work in harmony with children whom few adults could tolerate. Much thought and money are invested to make the surroundings so beautiful that the children can see the school considers them worthwhile human beings. In Bettelheim's opinion, equipping a treatment center with utilitarian but ugly furniture, chinaware and the like is the same as telling the patients, "We can't give you anything nice because you'll destroy it."

The school lets the children wreak havoc until they begin to feel secure. They are restrained from hurting themselves or other children physically, but there are no other rules. They may eat with their hands, dirty themselves, eliminate when and where they want to. They can also run away—often accompanied by a counselor who gives comfort and protection. From a psychotic youngster's wild rampages, as well as from his mute withdrawal into total inactivity or strange rituals, counselors gradually learn what went wrong in the child's past. The principal aim is to make relationships with people seem gratifying; the main tool is an attempt to satisfy all a child's needs, spoken and unspoken, tangible and intangible. At a concrete level, this means food above all else: snacks, especially candy, are always available.

One of the Orthogenic School's most touching cases is that of Joey, an autistic child whose mother acknowledged that at his birth she had "thought of him as a thing rather than a person." By the time he entered the school, at the age of nine, Joey's psychosis was so severe he had indeed almost become an object. He believed he was run by electrical machines, devices he himself built. To him, his constructions were vital life-support systems, and he took them everywhere. In the dining room he connected himself to a wall outlet with imaginary wires so his food would digest. All activities required similar connections. Even then, there was little he could do because his hands were always holding the contraptions that kept him alive. Slowly he allowed his counselors to understand the meaning of this behavior. In Bettelheim's words, "Since he felt excluded from the circle of humanity, he plugged himself into another circle that nourished—the electrical circuit."

After a long time, he began to identify himself with living things —eggs and chickens—instead of with machines. One day he hid under a table he had draped with blankets and then emerged with the triumphant statement: "I laid myself as an egg, hatched myself and gave birth to me." It was obvious that he had begun life all over. But he was almost 12 years old, with many lost years to make up. At first he drank from a bottle, ate baby food and played with childish toys. Over the next six years, he grew up emotionally, and when he was 18 and no longer psychotic, he went home to his parents, with whom he was by then able to form meaningful relationships. He finished high school and, using his gift for handling machinery, became a TV repairman.

Joey's rehabilitation belies the popular idea that psychosis is incurable. Still, recovery involves such dramatic change it seems like a miracle to both doctor and patient. The authority on psychosis Silvano Arieti noted that "therapists remember with great pleasure the feeling of joy and the atmosphere of festivity created when former schizophrenic patients come to visit them years after the end of treatment. Former psychotic patients never become index cards or collections of old data on yellowed medical records. They remain very much alive in the therapist's inner life to the end of his days."

Cultural bridge to treatment

The role that culture plays in the treatment of psychiatric disorders has been studied by experts since the 19th Century, when Western-trained physicians who were practicing in Africa and Asia found that patients did not respond to therapy effective in Europe. Such experiences suggested that a deliberate effort to supply the mentally ill with the hallmarks of their own culture—language, food, religion and folkways—would enhance the efficacy of conventional treatments.

That was the idea behind the establishment of the unique Xipe-Totec Mental Health Clinic in California in 1971. Named after the Aztec god of spring, a symbol of rebirth, the clinic was set up in a hospital ward that was decorated with murals of Latin American life, folk masks, carvings and representations of ancient Maya and Aztec gods (opposite).

The clinic, under the direction of Mexican-born psychiatric social worker Ignacio Aguilar, is intended for Mexican and Mexican-American patients. They are chosen for their adaptability to the program; drug addicts, alcoholics and violent individuals are excluded, as are persons of Latin American descent who resist being identified with their background.

For Mexicans or Mexican-Americans who qualify, the clinic's ethnically oriented program, with its deliberate emphasis on cultural heritage and customs, provides a friendly environment that makes patients receptive to individual treatment. Said Aguilar, "The program reassures them and makes each of them feel, 'Here is a place where I am going to get well.'"

Celebrating their cultural heritage, patients in Xipe-Totec clinic stamp through an exuberant Mexican dance. The painted figure at the clinic's entrance is Kukulcán, a Maya god of all good, traditionally depicted as a plumed serpent.

PHOTOGRAPHED BY BILL EPPRIDGE

122

Kukulcán
"Serpiente
Emplumada
de los M

Doing things the Mexican way

To establish a rapport with the patients, activities in the Xipe-Totec clinic are given a distinctly Latin American flavor. Dances are held to the rhythms of the Mexican hat dance or the merengue. There are readings of Spanish folklore or the poetry of contemporary South Americans. In crafts classes, the patients make plaster-of-paris molds of pre-Columbian figurines. On outings they visit Olvera Street, Los Angeles' historic Mexican district, or the Padua Hills Theater, where the city's Mexican colony puts on plays.

Within the ward, everyone is encouraged to express his feelings in ways that come naturally to him. The clinic often rings with the *grito,* a spontaneous shout of the Mexican that, says one therapist, "sounds like a thousand Apaches on the warpath."

In a crafts room festooned with versions of a Mexican religious hanging called ojo de dios (eye of God), clinic director Ignacio Aguilar shows a patient how to make his own ojo. When the patient finishes it, he will hang it over his bed, to remind him he is watched over by God.

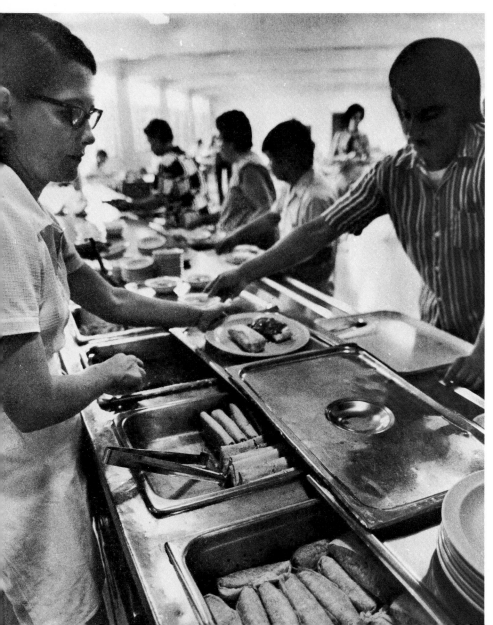

Absorbed in the music of his homeland, a patient listens as another strums. "Music is so important to the emotional nature of the Mexican," says Aguilar, "that some patients only come to life when they can play their guitars. And yet it is often not allowed in regular hospitals."

A patient picks up tamales—meat-filled pancakes—at the weekly lunch featuring Mexican food. From time to time the women patients prepare a fiesta meal of special Latin dishes to celebrate a birthday or the departure of a patient.

The death and life of Dolores

Culture not only shapes the environment at the Xipe-Totec clinic, to make patients feel at ease so they are easier to reach and treat, it also frequently influences the treatment. For a middle-aged woman named Dolores, clinic director Aguilar drew on Mexican ritual to solve a problem that itself arose in her Mexican-American background.

Dolores had split allegiances in a special sense. She had one child living in California, and three others living in Mexico. The children in both places wanted her to live with them, but she felt either choice would mean that she was abandoning a part of her family. The problem bothered her so much she eventually became depressed and sat in a chair all day, indifferent to everything around her. Aguilar had to resort to a drastic measure *(right)* to arouse her, and finally, to renew her interest in life he engaged her in purposeful play acting with a Mexican twist.

In an attempt to make Dolores respond, Aguilar sits down on top of her. "I'm going to use you as a nice soft armchair," he told her. "At least you're good for that." Moments later, Dolores reacted with a smile—and embraced him.

Acting out the conflicting pressures on Dolores, patients at the clinic play the roles of children pulling on their mother in a tug of war. The drama, which was repeated over several days, helped reconcile her to the division of her family.

In an enactment of a Mexican burial rite, patients put flowers on Dolores' "corpse." By treating her as if dead, Aguilar hoped to shock Dolores into awareness. After four hours she roused herself and gradually her symptoms abated.

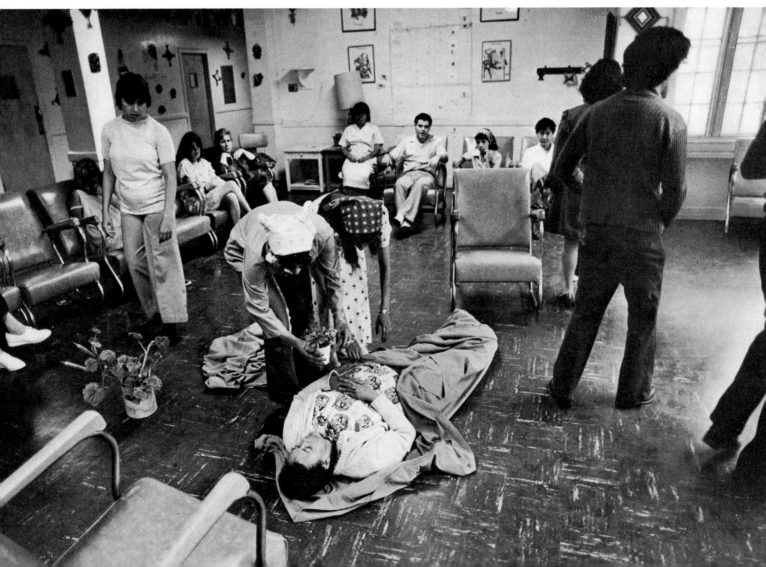

Succumbing to an attention-seeking impulse typical of her dissolute past, Maria takes off her dress, resisting the dissuasion of a clinic aide. Only when Aguilar ordered everyone to ignore her did she put her dress back on.

The conflicting roles of Maria

Aguilar's belief that the patient cannot be understood apart from his culture is demonstrated in the case of Maria, the young woman shown here. Maria was raised to revere the Virgin of Guadalupe, the patroness of all Mexicans. For her, the spiritual ideal of the Virgin is a realistic model for one's own life. Yet Maria was unable to follow the chaste ways of this ideal and had actually led a dissolute life. The conflict between her behavior and her religious values caused her great anguish, which Aguilar treated by a method related to her cultural background *(following pages)*.

Maria displays the ardor of her belief in the virtuous ways of her religion as she adds decorations to the clinic's shrine. She visited the shrine several times a day to pray and made endless vows; frequently she was moved to tears.

Finding a remedy in religion

"The Mexican's history—conquest by the Spaniards, subjugation under the Inquisition—has left him with a strong sense of fatalism," says Aguilar. "It is especially evident in the women, who are traditionally taught that it is their destiny to suffer and endure." By relating this expectation of pain to Maria's deep faith, Aguilar involved Maria in play acting *(opposite)* that made her feel she was being punished as required by her religion. The result was a release of painful feelings that brought emotional peace.

Riffling endlessly and aimlessly through snapshots of her children, Maria withdraws into a trancelike state. Aguilar surmised it was connected to guilt about the life she had been leading.

To give Maria the punishment she
yearned for, Aguilar directs her "stoning"
by the other patients, urging them to pelt
her with "rocks" made of newspaper
in an imitation of the penalty that ancient
Mosaic law demanded for such women.
Below, Maria sobs convulsively, atoning
for what she sees as her sins with
the pain of the symbolic stoning and the
discomfort of real public humiliation.

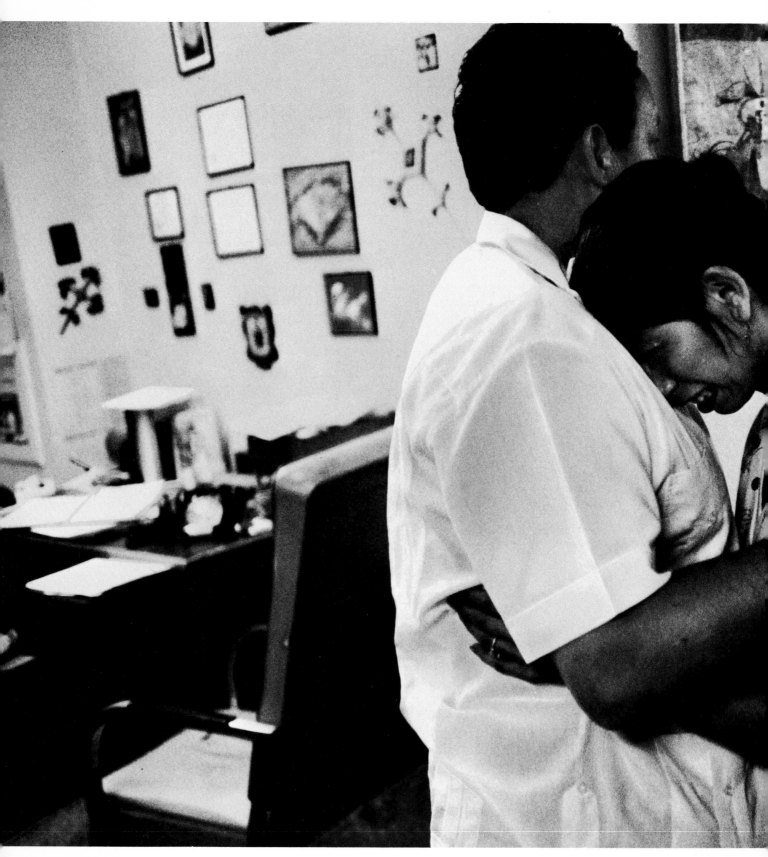

Purged of torment, Maria is comforted by Aguilar, who reassures her that everyone knows she is good and believes she will continue that way. "Remember what the Lord said: Go, and now sin no more," he told her. Maria replied, "Thank you," and he rejoined: "No, thank God."

Bold Departures

Q: Were you able to get a good night's sleep?
A: No.
Q: Why not?
A: There was the fear, always the fear you have in your mind, I suppose, that when you go to sleep maybe someone will jump on you during the night. They never did. But you think about those things. It was a lunatic asylum.

In these words Kenneth Donaldson described just one of the horrors he endured during the 15 years he spent in a mental hospital. A carpenter, divorced and the father of three children, Donaldson was 48 years old when, on a visit to his parents in 1957, he began complaining of harassment by unknown persons. Since he had suffered a mental breakdown several years earlier, his father became worried about these new signs and had him committed. The hospital was understaffed, with only one doctor for every 500 patients. Donaldson, living among convicted criminals and acutely deranged persons in a locked 60-bed ward, was given virtually no psychiatric treatment.

In 1970, having petitioned repeatedly and unsuccessfully for his freedom, he filed a suit on behalf of himself and other inmates, demanding that they either be treated or released and awarded damages. As it happened, the hospital did release Donaldson a year later, but the damage claim kept the case alive. In June 1975 the United States Supreme Court unanimously ruled that every nondangerous mental patient who is institutionalized involuntarily has the right either to be treated or released. Looking back at his hospital experience, Donaldson said, "It took 15 years out of my life without any legitimate reason. I made hundreds of friends who died there. They weren't any crazier than I was."

The ruling that gave Donaldson's story its bittersweet ending reflected a changing public attitude toward the mentally disturbed not only in the United States but also around the world. In place of the old prejudice that mocked and dismissed them as "crazy," there was recognition that victims of mental disorders, like other people, have human rights. And if they were not being wholeheartedly welcomed into all sectors of ordinary life, neither were they being indiscriminately consigned to impersonal institutions. Instead there was a growing tolerance toward them and, even more important, a willingness to reexamine their plight.

The reasons for this striking reversal were varied. Donaldson's confinement coincided with a time of profound cultural shock in many countries. Old notions of what constituted appropriate mores were challenged; formerly unconventional modes of thought, speech and dress gained social acceptance. By extension, this led to a less dogmatic view of the deviant behavior associated with mental disorders.

Of more direct moment to the mentally disturbed, the change in public attitude also stemmed from a new optimism concerning their potential for returning to normal life. This optimism was based on a series of extraordinary discoveries, begun just a few years before Donaldson entered his nightmare world and continuing to this day. Some of the discoveries revealed how the brain worked, and in doing so indicated what malfunctioning mechanisms might be the cause of mental disturbances. Other discoveries were the new drugs that seem to cure —or at least ameliorate—many kinds of psychiatric ailments. It was often possible to figure out how a particular drug worked—what physiological change it effected in the body—and this information provided more clues to the normal and abnormal operation of the brain.

Both the drug discoveries and the detailed understanding of brain mechanisms began in the decade after World War II. In the years following, one fact piled on another to support the first widely accepted theory to explain a physical basis for serious mental illness, schizophrenia in particular. It implicates an essential function of the mind—perception of the outside world—that is to a great extent controlled by one small section of the brain, a kind of master switch. This theory is far from proved; Soviet scientists, on a different tack, blamed mental disturbances on viruses after they found virus-like particles in the spinal fluid of schizophrenics. But the theory based on brain operation is attractive because it makes some kinds of irrational behavior—delusions of persecution, the hearing of voices—seem quite understandable. And its outlines fit well with what is known about the curative effects of such mind-altering drugs as tranquilizers, energizers and stimulants. To many authorities, this new theory signals the beginning of the end of the long search for physical defects underlying psychological ailments.

The two men who initiated the breakthrough—an Italian, Giuseppe Moruzzi, and an American, Horace Magoun—were not looking for clues

Kenneth Donaldson, an ex-carpenter, established a mental patient's right to live his own life in the United States. Confined to a mental hospital for nearly 15 years after complaining of harassment by unknown people, Donaldson sued for freedom. In a landmark ruling, the U.S. Supreme Court held that nondangerous mental patients may not be detained without treatment against their will.

to mental illness. They were physiologists with a special interest in the nervous system, and at the time, in 1949, they were trying to learn more about the nerve impulses that stream into the cerebral cortex, the thinking part of the brain. These impulses carry messages from all over the body: from the sense organs—the organs of sight, hearing, smell, touch and taste—and from every muscle except those that move by reflex action. The messages arrive in countless numbers; the amount of information involved is prodigious. The signal-laden nerve impulses —tiny bursts of electricity that travel along nerve fibers—take different routes to the cortex, depending on where they originate. Some go directly to the cortex; others branch off into other parts of the brain, ultimately reaching the cortex after a series of often complicated relays.

Moruzzi and Magoun, working at Northwestern University in Illinois, decided to try to trace some of these circuits. They simulated the action of nerve impulses by applying electrical charges to parts of the brain known to send impulses to the cortex. Using cats as subjects, they attached an electrode to a particular part of the brain and sent an electrical charge through it. Soon they were concentrating on the brain stem, which rises from the top of the spinal cord to the center of the brain.

In the case of the human brain, the stem is shaped like a thick spear of broccoli, with a bulbous top. Within the stem is a segment about the shape and size of a finger. Called the reticular formation (*reticulum* is Latin for network), this segment is marked by intricate tracery; it is, indeed, a network—of nerve fibers. Moruzzi and Magoun sent electricity through an electrode attached to the reticular formation of a sleeping cat. The cat promptly awoke—not with a violent start, but peacefully, as if it had awakened normally. The experiment was repeated on other cats, with the same result.

That the artificial signal from the reticular formation produced the same effect on the brain as normal awakening was established with the aid of the electroencephalograph, or EEG, an instrument that measures and records electrical activity within the brain, so-called brain waves. EEG studies had already revealed that distinctive brain-wave patterns were characteristic of sleep and wakefulness. One pattern changes into another as a person falls asleep or wakes up. Moruzzi and Magoun recorded the brain waves of sleeping cats when they were awakened normally, then compared those recordings with measurements made when they were awakened artificially by an electrical jolt through the reticular formation; the brain-wave changes were identical. It seemed likely that sleep and wakefulness were controlled normally by natural signals from the reticular formation.

This area within the brain stem, Moruzzi and Magoun concluded, served as an arousal system, putting the thinking brain into a state of alert, so it could respond to signals from its sense organs. Accordingly, they gave the reticular formation a new name: reticular activating system, or RAS. Other scientists—particularly those who had been investigating the psychological effects of sensory stimulation (and its lack), soon made the connection between the Moruzzi-Magoun discovery and mental disturbance. Their research had already shown that lack of stimulation—blindfolding and muffling people so they could see, feel and hear nothing—can cause hallucinations strikingly similar to those of mental disturbance.

Hallucinations are, of course, failures of perception. And sensory perception obviously depends on arousal: in sleep sensory signals are essentially cut off; in wakefulness they are received in varying degree depending on the alertness of the mind. If the RAS controls the stages of arousal from sleep to maximum alertness, it must influence sensory perception. A malfunction in RAS circuits could make the mind either too sensitive or too insensitive to sensory signals and is thus one physical failure that could cause misperception. The same effect would result, of course, if other circuits not directly connected to the RAS brought the mind too many or too few signals. It turns out that the two kinds of breakdown are similar, involving the transmission of nerve signals. Faulty transmission floods the brain with more data than it can handle or deprives it of needed data. It seems to cause the hallucinations so characteristic of mental ills.

This implication of the RAS in mental disorder has been supported by further research that shows how this part of the brain acts as a master switch. It not only controls the flow of signals from the senses to the thinking brain, but also adjusts the attention that the brain gives the signals. As nerve impulses originating in the sensory organs pass through the brain stem en route to the cortex above, they branch into the RAS. The RAS then sends up its own signals, informing the cortex that the impulses are on the way. The RAS also monitors the impulses, telling the cortex which of the incoming signals are important.

This function of the RAS is critical. Although the cortex registers all of the myriad messages it receives, not all of them are urgent or even relevant. Only some require attention at any given time. If, for example, a hiker came in sight of a stand of spruces, a nerve impulse from his eyes would send that information to the cortex. But it would be of considerably less import than the information, sent simultaneously from the same organ, that the hiker had spotted a bear among the trees. The

Less work for hospitals

The number of mental patients who had to remain in U.S. hospitals was cut in half within just two decades after the introduction of modern psychiatric drugs. From a 1955 peak of 558,922 in institutions operated by state and county governments, where the great majority of the severely mentally ill are treated, the patient population dropped to 215,573 in 1974 *(below)*. Most of that remnant were long-term patients.

Number (in thousands) of resident patients
in U.S. state and county mental hospitals

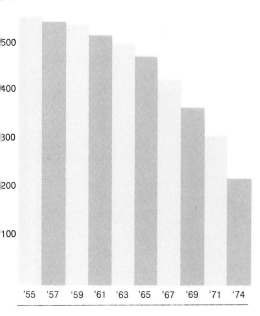

RAS, by monitoring the impulses, enables the cortex to focus its attention on the more relevant message and interpret it properly.

The traffic of messages between RAS and cortex is not one-way. The cortex signals back to the RAS guidance on how to monitor incoming signals. When the cortex has had an excess of information, it tells the RAS to stop alerting. Or it can order the RAS to favor some signals over others —play down the beauties of spruces in favor of more about that bear. The two-way traffic travels on parallel tracks. One set of tracks conveys activating impulses from the RAS up to the cortex. The other conveys inhibiting impulses from the cortex down to the RAS. The result is a state of attentiveness that permits the individual to make an efficient response to one particular message among many.

The most common example of this remarkable human capacity is the "cocktail-party effect." Almost everyone has experienced it. In the midst of a crowd of people, all talking to one another, an individual has no difficulty hearing the conversation he wants to hear and screening out all the others—as well as such noises as the tinkle of glasses and the whoops of the reveler who has downed his fourth Scotch. Despite this hubbub, he can even pick out his own name spoken across the room.

This capacity seems to be missing in some psychotics. Many schizophrenics lose the normal ability to disregard certain sensory perceptions while focusing their attention on what they want to or need to. As one recovered patient recalled: "Every face in the windows of a passing streetcar would be engraved on my mind, all of them concentrating on me and trying to pass me some sort of message." Schizophrenics, in short, experience a kind of sensory torrent: rather than tuning out needless data, they accept the entire sensory input indiscriminately. The result is chaos.

With the realization that such symptoms might reflect a biochemical malfunction in the attention mechanism of the RAS, doctors who deal with schizophrenics took a new look at the disorder. They reached a startling conclusion: that seemingly strange behavior of a patient is often a logical attempt to cope with the world as the patient experiences it. He tries to rationalize an overwhelming flood of perceptions and comes up with a delusion—an irrational answer.

One patient was capable of behaving quietly and sociably during some meals in the hospital cafeteria; yet during other meals he would grow livid with rage and excitement. Doctors found that in the first instance he ate with a single companion; in the second instance, other persons also shared the table. The change for the worse in the man's behavior, the doctors concluded, might be the result of the failure of the

A schizophrenic's view of the world

Many authorities now believe that an important factor in certain psychoses may be the brain's RAS, or reticular activating system, which helps to screen sensory impressions coming into the mind. Normally it sorts out one intelligible impression and passes it along to the cortex, which coordinates activities of mind and body; but in the psychotic's RAS, as illustrated by the pictures below, it may be passing along a flood of unfiltered impressions, causing him to be hopelessly confused.

A schizophrenic walking down the street, for example, may think that the buildings are jumping up and down. In a crowded room he may find that it is impossible to screen out a particular conversation. Recent research suggests that schizophrenics who complain of these bizarre effects may simply have malfunctioning RAS circuits.

As the man at left walks along the street, his body moves and his eyes register a series of images of the buildings. But his reticular activating system screens most of these impressions (red dots) and passes one clear continuous impression (green dot) to the cortex. In the schizophrenic (right) the RAS gives a green light to all impressions, and he perceives the buildings as a series of images.

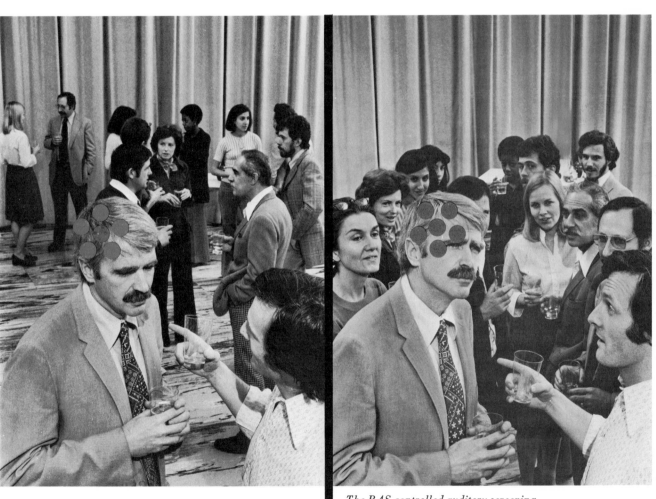

The RAS-controlled auditory screening process called the cocktail-party effect is working properly at left, as the RAS allows the voice of the close conversational companion to go through (green dot), effectively obscuring all other voices (red dots). At right the RAS of the schizophrenic fails to do its screening job, transmitting all of the voices to the cortex in a jumble.

cocktail-party effect; his RAS apparently did not help him sort out the greater number of sounds at the table. He gave the doctors a perfectly logical summary of the reasons for his frustration. "When people are talking I just get scraps of it," he said. "If it is just one person who is speaking that's not so bad but if the others join in then I can't pick it up at all. I just can't get into time with that conversation. It makes me feel open—as if things are closing in on me and I have lost control."

The sense of sight as well as hearing can be affected. In one hospital a patient habitually walked with his hands cupped around his eyes, using them as blinders are used on horses. Asked why he shielded his eyes in this way, he explained he was trying to adjust to "the movement of the earth." The answer baffled the doctors until they linked the patient's way of walking to a real problem with his field of vision. Walking, of course, changes any walker's field of vision, filling it with a procession of moving images as his head and body bob up and down. Normally, people automatically ignore the moving images. But this patient could not, according to the current hypothesis, screen out the movements, and he took them all in indiscriminately. It seemed to him the earth itself was moving. Such an effect could plausibly occur as the result of a malfunctioning RAS. By shielding his eyes—thus narrowing his field of vision—he was trying to maintain his balance.

Another patient walked with a slow, hesitant gait, frequently halting to stare down at his feet. "When I move quickly," he explained, "it's a strain on me. Things go too quick for my mind. . . . It's as if you were seeing a picture one moment and another picture the next. I just stop and watch my feet. Everything is all right if I stop, but if I start moving again I lose control." From this and other information, doctors theorized that a schizophrenic not only fails to distinguish between relevant and irrelevant sensory data but also finds it difficult to absorb data that may come at too fast a rate for him. The more quickly this patient moved, the bigger and swifter the barrage of sights he encountered. This proved intolerable unless he slowed down and took periodic rest stops. Fixing his gaze down on his feet also helped; he was thus able to shut out most of the disturbing stimuli around him.

Some of these failures in perception could result from a breakdown in the two-way traffic between RAS and cortex, a disruption in the stimulating signals being sent up while inhibiting signals are sent back. If some of these transmission channels were interrupted, the cortex would either be understimulated or overwhelmed. Failures in other transmission channels, separate from the RAS-cortex connections, could have a similar effect if the RAS proved unable to adjust the brain sufficiently to compensate for their malfunctioning.

All the paths nerve impulses travel, whether between RAS and cortex or anywhere else in the body, are constructed the same way. They are made up of cells interspersed by spaces called synapses. A nerve impulse must jump across these gaps to get from cell to cell and on to its destination. It cannot make the jump without help from a "neurotransmitter," a chemical substance produced by each cell. The cell releases the neurotransmitter into the synapses, and its presence there activates the adjoining cell, enabling the impulse to go on its way. In various parts of the nervous system, chemical substances—perhaps 11 different kinds—serve as neurotransmitters.

But something may go wrong with a neurotransmitter. Normally, after a nerve impulse has gone by, the neurotransmitter is reabsorbed into the cell that released it; then it is released again into the synapse to help the next impulse on its way. For reasons not yet fully understood, a neurotransmitter sometimes fails to be reabsorbed by its cell and so cannot be employed again. The next impulse to come along gets no help at all; it stops dead at the gap, unable to proceed on its journey.

The trouble this may cause in the RAS-cortex linkup is twofold. If an activating signal from the RAS is blocked on its way to the cortex, the RAS cannot clue the cortex to the impending arrival of a message. If an inhibiting signal from the cortex cannot get back to the RAS, the cortex cannot tell the RAS to stop alerting, in effect, to cut something off. The RAS keeps sending its signals, adding to the overload of information in the cortex. Under this burden, it becomes virtually impossible for the cortex to focus attention on particular messages.

Such transmission-channel breakdowns have been related not only to the hallucinations and delusions of schizophrenia but also to other aspects of mental disturbance. Sleeplessness is one example. For years it was thought that the insomnia that usually accompanies a breakdown was simply a symptom of the trouble. In the late 1960s, scientists began to suspect that it might, in fact, be a cause. Anyone who wakes at 3 a.m. and cannot get back to sleep is likely to begin stewing over some problem. If this happens often enough, the researchers reasoned, even a healthy person could persuade himself he is suffering from some buried emotional conflict. Worried and confused, he may become ill in truth, when all he may need to restore his sense of well-being is enough healthy sleep—that is, the kind in which the stages of light and deep sleep follow a more normal pattern than that induced by sleeping pills.

Control over sleep is a function of the RAS—when it stops sending arousal signals, the cortex goes to sleep. What makes it stop are two neurotransmitters. This knowledge might be applied, researchers believe, to block illness by restoring normal sleep with the very neurotransmitters that turn the RAS off. Injecting the transmitters themselves does not work, but it may be possible to synthesize "sleep juices"—compounds transformed by the body into neurotransmitters. One promising substance is tryptophane, a natural component of meat and milk, which is converted by the body into serotonin, the transmitter that induces light sleep. An effective sleep juice, however, would also have to include something to regulate norepinephrine, the transmitter that causes deep sleep, since both stages of sleep are needed for normal slumber. The new theories about the physical causes of mental illness rest on the assumption that what goes wrong affects the operation of neurotransmitters (even when other compounds are implicated, the belief is that they probably influence the generation and absorption of transmitters). This assumption is not plucked out of the air. Much of the evidence supporting the theories arises from research on the curative mechanisms of new drugs, and they seem to work by either increasing or decreasing

the action of transmitters. This knowledge is relatively recent, and it was hard won. It caps a search for mental remedies as painful and drawn out as the search for causes—and until the middle of this century, mostly as fruitless.

It seems that nearly every substance in the world has been tried, at one time or another in one place or another, as a cure for mental disturbance. From a modern perspective, some of the cures appear a good deal more irrational than the conditions they purported to heal. In 16th Century Europe a popular antidote for melancholia, taken orally by victims, was an Arabian import called the bezoar stone—actually a stone extracted from the gall bladder of a goat. The stones were in such demand that unscrupulous apothecaries enriched themselves by substituting pebbles for the genuine article. In England, from medieval times to the early 19th Century, the diet of sufferers from nervous disorders was supplemented by usnea, a common moss—except that the moss prescribed in this case was scraped from the skulls of criminals who had been hung in chains and left to die. The theory was that the gruesome nature of the usnea's source of supply would have a shocking and hence therapeutic effect on the patient's system.

Probably the oldest prescription for mental ills, and the most enduring, has been alcohol. Employed both to calm the manic and to enliven the depressed, it was used as early as 6400 B.C. in Mesopotamia. In Greece 6,000 years later, Hippocrates was prescribing wine laced with the juice of a mandrake root as treatment for either anxiety or depression. Two millennia later, in 19th Century America, women in the throes of what was called "nervous prostration" perked themselves up with Lydia Pinkham's Vegetable Compound, which in its original version was a blend of herbs heavily laced with alcohol.

Next to alcohol, opiates were the main nostrum of the past. Such drugs, which deaden anxiety and induce euphoria, were used to combat depression as far back as the Seventh Century B.C., when opium was taken in lozenge or liquid form—or sometimes sniffed—by Assyrian victims of the ailment. After opium's derivative, morphine, was isolated in Germany in 1803, it quickly gained favor as an antidepressant, and so did cocaine when it was isolated from Peruvian coca leaves in the 1850s. The trouble with opiates, of course, was that they replaced one ill with another: melancholics turned into dope addicts.

Not all the old remedies were as dangerous as opiates or as ridiculous as bezoar stones. Some worked better than many people realized. For centuries the people of Africa and India had used the snakeroot plant, *Rauwolfia serpentina*, as a kind of panacea. It was employed in

This relaxed session, held over lunch, is part of a distinctive approach to mental illnesses at the Arbours Association Crisis Center in London. The informal setting is part of a deliberate effort to ease the anxiety of a person caught in a mental crisis, so that therapists can establish contact and get to understand him, then help him solve problems one by one.

treating everything from snakebite and fevers to hysteria and other mental upsets. It turned up in London in 1925, when a visiting Nigerian cabinet minister suffered a severe psychotic breakdown. After no British doctor could help him, a cable was sent requesting the services of a Nigerian healer, Chief Adetona. Brought to London, the chief administered rauwolfia, accompanied by the appropriate tribal incantations, and the patient soon recovered.

At the time nobody but the Nigerians paid much attention. Not until a quarter of a century later did chemists J. M. Miller, E. Schlittler and H. J. Bein of the Ciba Pharmaceutical Company in Switzerland, as part of a routine survey of exotic plants with reputed therapeutic properties, check out rauwolfia for its value in treating high blood pressure. In 1952 they extracted from it a drug named reserpine, which proved to be an effective tranquilizer—but almost simultaneously in France came the discovery of another and better tranquilizer, chlorpromazine. The modern era of psychiatric treatment had begun.

The discovery of chlorpromazine, still the drug of choice for schizophrenia, came about as a result of a chain of events reaching back to 1880. In that year a German chemist synthesized a drug to treat worm infections in the gastrointestinal tract; he named it phenothiazine. A number of phenothiazine derivatives were developed over the years. One of them, promethazine, was a member of the so-called antihistamine family of drugs, widely celebrated as a treatment for the common cold, and also used to remedy lowered blood pressure and shock.

It occurred to a French surgeon, Henri Laborit, that promethazine might solve a problem that had long worried him: when patients about to undergo operations were given a general anesthetic, they not only became unconscious but sometimes suffered fatal shock when their blood pressure sank too low. Promethazine, Laborit thought, might temper the shock effect of the anesthetic. When he tried it on preoperative patients, he found they were calm, relaxed, and only somewhat drowsy; even after a major operation they were "never excited."

French drug chemists went to work to develop phenothiazine drugs. One of them was chlorpromazine. Laborit found that it was even more effective than promethazine. It kept the preoperative patient not only calm but also alert. In fact, Laborit reported: "It did not cause any loss in consciousness, nor lead to any change in the patient's mental agility, but made him slightly sleepy and, above all, disinterested in what was going on around him."

Laborit himself foresaw the potential for calming confused and agitated psychiatric patients, and he passed along the drug to several

continued on page 151

At the daily Unitas council, ghetto children and their teen-age "parents" gather round the "family circle." Although some are so emotionally troubled they cannot bring themselves to join the circle, Dr. Edward Eismann (standing) tries to include all in opening rituals that emphasize the sense of belonging; he catches everyone's eye in turn and explains that all of them are there "as a family to help each other."

Therapy in the street

Mental illness breeds in the streets of the slums, and that is where Dr. Edward Eismann of New York's Lincoln Community Mental Health Center undertook to combat it. On the premise that much disturbance stems from the lack of a warm, enduring social framework of family and friends, he set out to remedy that lack on the concrete and asphalt of Fox Street in the impoverished South Bronx. There Dr. Eismann created Unitas (Unity), a new sort of family in which children can benefit from an intimacy they otherwise might never experience. The group includes both normal and troubled youngsters (no distinction is made between them

except to conceal from outsiders the real names of the disturbed children).

To nurture the sense of family, the daily council (above) was established, providing a forum where problems of life together could be aired. For the more disturbed children in the group individual attention was provided by teenage volunteers recruited in the neighborhood. Each of the older "parents" was trained to work with only one child (overleaf), talking to him, playing with him, holding him, even feeding him. All this took place on familiar ground with familiar people—creating, in Dr. Eismann's words, "a natural system within which the community can heal itself."

147

*While Dr. Eismann starts to calm the boy
he refers to as Alex, a teen-age "parent"
settles a tense situation with Alex's
brother (left). Both brothers suffered from
uncontrolled rages, which Dr. Eismann
is shown treating with reassurance
and physical restraint—firm hugging.*

In one of his frequent rages, Alex is held by his "parent," Maria, and another teen-age counselor in what Dr. Eismann calls "a human strait jacket of loving arms." Simultaneously, Maria soothes Alex's rage by comforting him and assuring him that he can control himself.

After some weeks in Unitas, Alex, his rages reduced to three or four a day, plays happily at rope skipping—an activity that demands cooperation and controls he could not provide before he joined.

Encircled by two pairs of arms, Alex is
fed milk as Dr. Eismann teaches Maria a
procedure he considers crucial:
the placing of food in a child's mouth by
the hands of someone who loves him.
Maria mothers Alex like a baby, giving
him, with food, emotional sustenance
that he could not previously accept.

psychiatrists in Paris. When they tried it on their patients—in 1952 only a year after it had been synthesized—they found the behavior of schizophrenics was transformed dramatically. Newly serene, no longer given to bizarre acts and uncontrollable outbursts, the patients became able to function in normal society.

A second family of antischizophrenic drugs, introduced in 1958, are the butyrophenones. Unlike the phenothiazines, they were developed specifically to combat psychosis by pharmacologist Paul Janssen of Belgium. They proved to be as effective as the phenothiazines and had fewer side effects. These compounds are all called tranquilizers because they reduce arousal. They relieve anxiety so that, in an old-fashioned sense, they "calm the nerves." They do not eradicate mental quirks directly but make them less worrisome, so the mind can more readily get a grasp on reality. In some cases the effect is amazing; a patient who has been talking to himself and jumping around becomes quiet and responsive after taking pills for a few weeks, able to carry on a rational conversation and to resume a reasonably normal life.

Oddly enough, the compounds called tranquilizers also revive psychotics who seem to be too tranquil—so withdrawn that they sit perfectly still and do not say a word. These people are not necessarily suffering from depression; they apparently are withdrawn because they cannot cope with overarousal. The tranquilizers seem to help them by reducing the overwhelming flood of sensory perception to a level at which it can be dealt with rationally.

Tranquilizers rebalance an overaroused mind toward quiet. But underarousal is also a common occurrence in psychosis, making patients withdrawn, uncommunicative and depressed. To rebalance minds tipped in that direction, drugs called energizers, or antidepressants, were discovered in 1957.

Antidepressant drugs sound as if they should be stimulants, like "pep pills," but they are not. A stimulant imparts a quick charge, turning an individual's mood from normal to euphoric. Antidepressants do not affect the normal state of mind but slowly raise a depressed mood to a normal one; the change may not even be noticeable for about two weeks.

The two major types of antidepressants—the tricyclic drugs and the monoamine oxidase (MAO) inhibitors—were discovered almost simultaneously. In 1957, Nathan Kline of Rockland State Hospital in New York, who had been looking for evidence of an "opposite number" to tranquilizers, noticed the strange effects of a drug, iproniazid, that had been introduced earlier to treat tuberculosis. It had the unexpected result of markedly lifting patients' spirits. It and related compounds known as MAO inhibitors were used as antidepressants for a time but have since been replaced by another class of substances discovered in the same year. These were the tricyclics, synthesized by a Swiss group headed by Roland Kuhn. They had been looking for a sedative but came upon an energizer that seemed as if it might counteract psychotic depressions.

All these drugs were found and put to use before anyone knew how they worked, although their obvious influence on mental activity suggested that they somehow affected the neurotransmitters relaying signals in the brain. In the 1960s a number of investigators began to pile up evidence supporting this idea, but perhaps the most convincing demonstration of the drug mechanism, and thus of the basis of psychosis, came from research on drugs that are now seldom employed to treat mental illness: the amphetamines.

The first amphetamine, called Benzedrine, was developed in 1932 by Gordon Alles, a California chemist, as a medicine for asthma. Trying it himself, Alles noted it had a euphoric effect. This led to the synthesis of a variety of pep pills and their use not only by soldiers during World War II to overcome exhaustion, but also, in the postwar era, by all sorts of healthy people to get the extra lift they thought they needed.

The amphetamines were found to be addictive and fell into disfavor among psychiatrists, but the symptoms of the addicts attracted attention. They acted psychotic, leading one investigator, Solomon H. Snyder, to call amphetamine a kind of schizophrenia-producing machine. "Amphetamine psychosis is the only drug psychosis known," wrote Snyder, "which so closely resembles schizophrenia, of the acute paranoid type, that patients are regularly misdiagnosed as schizophrenics." To clinch the parallel, Snyder pointed out that both schizophrenia and amphetamine psychosis were relieved by phenothiazine tranquilizers. Since amphetamine was known to stimulate the central nervous system, the conclusion seemed obvious: "It is the alert, centrally stimulated features of the paranoid schizophrenic's mental apparatus which probably provoke him to strive for an intellectual framework in which to focus all the strange feelings that are coming over him as the psychosis develops. This quest for meaning and its subsequent 'discovery' in a system of delusions might be the essence of the paranoid process in these patients."

His deduction was based on research by a number of scientists. Using radioactive compounds—and a unique staining method developed in Sweden that made certain neurotransmitters visible as a fluorescent green when brain sections were examined under a microscope—re-

Ups and downs of drugs

Of the drugs commonly prescribed to tip the balance of the mind—stimulants and antidepressants to energize it, tranquilizers and sedatives to calm it—those of moderate strength *(middle of chart, below)* are most used in rebalancing disturbed minds toward normality. But too much of any type, whether it excites the mind or calms it, brings the same end result: death.

EXTREME STIMULATION

DRUG	EFFECTS
DEATH	
	Coma
	Convulsions
Stimulants amphetamines	Anxiety
	Excitement
Antidepressants MAO inhibitors: Marplan, Nardil, Niamid	
tricyclic compounds: Tofranil, Pertofrane, Norpramin	Mood elevation
lithium	
Tranquilizers Minor meprobamate: Equanil, Miltown chlordiazepoxide hydrochloride: Librium diazepam: Valium	Relief of anxiety; relaxation of tension
Major butyrophenone: Haldol phenothiazines chlorpromazine: Thorazine, Chlor-PZ reserpine: Serpasil, Rau-Sed	Reduction of psychotic overactivity
Sedatives barbiturates	Drowsiness and sleep
	Impaired judgment
	Convulsions
	Coma
DEATH	

EXTREME DEPRESSION

searchers found that amphetamine stimulates by increasing the supply of the neurotransmitter dopamine; presumably schizophrenics suffer from an excess of dopamine. Tranquilizers counteract the symptoms of both schizophrenics and amphetamine addicts by blocking the action of the excess dopamine. In a similar way, the causes of depression were traced to an insufficiency of two other transmitters, norepinephrine and serotonin, which are increased by antidepressants.

Thus far, the actions in mental disturbance of only these three transmitters—serotonin, norepinephrine and dopamine—have been identified, although at least eight other compounds are also known to carry nerve signals. All three seem to have important roles in one or more of the circuits connecting the RAS and cortex. This evidence has suggested to many scientists that there may be a remarkably simple basis for most mental illness: breakdowns in signal circuits resulting in too much or too little information for the mind to handle.

The human benefits of this work of the 1950s and 1960s can be read in statistics. Most of the severely mentally ill now need hospital care only briefly—often in a general hospital rather than an asylum; then they can return to the outside world. The recurrent nature of these ailments may lead to repeated hospitalization, but even this is preferable to permanent isolation from society. Of the minority still doomed to a lifetime of psychosis, most are the senile elderly or middle-aged patients confined so long they have been made incurable not by the basic nature of their illnesses but by the effects of institutionalization.

Statistics alone, despite the dramatic story they tell, cannot reveal all dimensions of the mid-20th Century revolution in the prospects for the mentally disturbed. The public's attitude toward mental disorders has been transformed as rising numbers of families and friends and neighbors have direct proof that a schizophrenic released from hospital bondage, or a depressive relieved of his grim burden, can get along in the normal world. A liberalizing trend has swept away old yardsticks for measuring what was, or was not, "correct" or "proper" in human behavior. Many formerly taboo topics, among them the subject of mental illness, are now frankly discussed. Brought into the open, mental disorders no longer seem as terrifying as before. In some cases what had been considered abnormal behavior became normal and acceptable.

Perhaps the most striking indication of significant change was the shift in attitude in America toward homosexuality. Up until the early 1970s, homosexuality was defined as a mental illness by the American Psychiatric Association. Homosexuals felt that the characterization was prejudice rather than a reflection of objective scientific fact. A six-year campaign on their part ended in victory in December of 1973, when the APA's 13-member board of trustees voted unanimously to remove homosexuality from the association's roster of mental illnesses.

In the wake of the APA vote, a study made by the Institute for Sex Research at Indiana University in 1974 indicated that 86 per cent of male homosexuals in the United States felt no need for, and did not want, psychiatric treatment. They believed they should continue in their chosen way of life. Some members of the psychiatric community—behavior therapists in particular—have responded to this viewpoint by rethinking their attitudes. In 1967, Gerald C. Davison of the State University of New York had developed a behavior-modification technique, popularized as the "Playboy therapy," that was intended to turn male homosexuals into heterosexuals by such means as showing them pictures of voluptuous nudes from *Playboy* magazine. But only seven years later, in 1974, Davison repudiated his own therapy and all others designed to alter the sexual preferences of homosexuals. Many of his colleagues, he reported, now would be willing to work to "help their homosexual clients adjust more satisfactorily to a permanent homosexual identity."

It is easy to overestimate the extent of such changes in attitude toward behavior that had not been considered normal. Most people retain some fear and distrust of the mentally ill. In the summer of 1972, a political sensation was caused in the United States by the disclosure that Senator Thomas P. Eagleton, Democratic candidate for Vice President, had been hospitalized three times for depression and had received shock treatments twice. A national poll of voters showed that a majority thought that, despite his medical history, he was qualified for the office —only 19 per cent thought he was not and 28 per cent said they had no opinion. Even so, he was forced to withdraw his candidacy. However, the voters of his home state of Missouri did not lose faith in him. When he ran for reelection to the United States Senate two years later, he won 60 per cent of the vote—9 per cent more than in his first victory. Clearly, Missourians had no qualms about being represented in Washington by a man who had experienced three serious sieges of depression.

The most encouraging result of changes in public attitude and improvements in therapy is a clear trend toward more humanitarian—and more effective—treatment of the mentally ill. The efficacy of the new drugs prompted the emptying of many institutions, the transfer of medical care for crisis cases to general hospitals and the establishment of "halfway house" schemes to help people who had been psychotic to ease their way back into normal life.

In 1972 there were only 19 psychiatrists in North Dakota, and the state's mental health association decided to augment their ranks by training as "mental health helpers" two groups to whom people normally tell their troubles—bartenders and hairdressers. In special classes (below), they learned to give upbeat, sympathetic advice. Then, armed with directories telling where their customers could get professional help, they went back to shaking cocktails (left) and curling hair with their helpful new skill.

Britain pioneered this new approach in the 1950s, setting up an extensive system to look after patients leaving hospital care. Many go back to live with their families. But for those who have lost touch with friends and families, there are a variety of living arrangements, some more supervised than others. As a first step for patients leaving psychiatric wards of general hospitals, there are hospital day areas, where the patient, still spending his nights in the hospital ward, is more or less unrestricted during the day and on weekends. After he is discharged from either a general hospital or mental institution, he may be treated at an outpatient clinic—or may stop by once a week or so, simply to let the doctors know how he feels. For those who have nowhere to live after their medical discharge, there are short-term hostels supervised by psychiatric social workers. There are long-term homes, with social worker staffs, for those who can hold jobs but probably can never cope quite on their own. Supervised lodgings—the social workers look in on them at intervals—are available for those who have readjusted to normal life fairly well and may later find their own places to live. Finally, group homes provide shared apartments that help eliminate the isolation of living alone. A patient may reside in a succession of such halfway houses until he can strike out independently and resume an essentially ordinary place in society.

The British had hoped this scheme would eliminate any need for institutions housing lifetime patients. It has not. The difficulties of providing effective supervision and treatment for all patients in scattered, small groups has modified optimism, although the commitment to community care for the mentally ill remains. One group of experts said, "We strongly support the concept of community care." Another report admitted the problems: "Experience continues to show the difficulty or impossibility of keeping some patients, mostly severely disabled schizophrenics and brain-damaged people, out of hospital. They may make impossible demands on their families, their GPs, and the social services; they may drift from one area to another, joining the ranks of the homeless and the vagrants. Many of them are ill-suited to the increasingly competitive and acquisitive conditions of urban life."

In the United States the half-way house theory was initially bolstered by the enthusiastic support of President Kennedy, and its acceptance spread. But construction of the houses lagged: in 1974 there were only about 200 across the nation. In their absence, some states have taken to placing formerly hospitalized patients in private proprietary homes or sleazy hotels, where they often receive only indifferent custodial care. Many suffer relapses and, wandering pathetically through the streets, come to be regarded as nuisances by residents. Local pressure can then send them back to the hospital. A more promising American development is the building of community mental health centers to take the place of the old hospitals. By 1974 there were 540 centers, with a total of 2,000 envisioned by 1980. They are intended to meet the entire mental health needs of a community of anywhere from 50,000 to 150,000 residents. Complexes that encompass a hospital, an outpatient clinic, a day-care center and an emergency unit, they offer treatment for all types of mental disorders, including alcoholism and drug addiction, and provide individual or group psychotherapy, as well as drug medication. The centers also maintain ties with welfare agencies, neighborhood organizations, police, ministers and private doctors, in an effort to wage all-out war against environmental factors that may contribute to mental illness.

For those people who return to their communities to make their way on their own after an experience in institutionalized living, the smoothness of the transition directly depends on the nature of their reception. They are not always received without reservation. A great deal hinges on whether they are harmless, a matter that psychiatrists cannot accurately predict. But in spite of occasional suspicion, most communities accept the mentally ill. As for the communities that are resistant, often all that is necessary in order that their citizens experience a change of heart is simple human contact.

A case in point is the Austrian town of Klagenfurt. In 1974, when the local psychiatric hospital became overcrowded, officials began literally to farm out their less disturbed patients. They placed them in small inns and farms, where they could do simple chores in exchange for their board. At first the townspeople were indignant, protesting that they wanted no "idiots" in their midst; even the innkeepers and farmers who housed the patients were reserved and cautious with their new boarders. But as everyone came to know the patients, reserve melted, to be replaced by affection and even respect. And the patients did so well that medical workers visited them only once a week.

At the end of the test period, not one of the boarding homes wanted to quit the program, and the patients are now boarded on a year-round basis. The Klagenfurters had learned what was learned centuries ago by the Belgian town of Geel *(overleaf)*, which for 500 years has had a similar system of caring for the mentally ill: by generating a more tolerant and more humane spirit in a community, the mental patient adds an extra dimension to its life.

A hometown for the mentally ill

Continuing an old tradition, a mental patient (tall youth, center) strolls through the marketplace of Geel with townspeople. Geelites tease strangers by saying, "I bet you cannot tell us apart."

Caring for the mentally ill in the everyday atmosphere of foster homes, as part of the routine of normal community life, is the newest trend in psychiatry, replacing a century and a half of emphasis on institutional treatment. The approach is rapidly spreading in Europe, North America and Africa.

The model for such family therapy is more than five centuries old. It survives today in the Belgian town of Geel, whose residents provide humane, effective care by taking disturbed people into their families.

The Flemish town's association with the mentally ill traces its beginnings to 600 A.D. According to legend an Irish king, seized by an incestuous lust for his daughter, pursued her to Geel. When his advances were refused, he beheaded the princess. She became a martyr and subsequently was acclaimed a patron saint of the emotionally ill. Pilgrims brought their disturbed relatives to her shrine at Geel and the townspeople began taking them into their homes, first as temporary boarders but in many cases permanently, as lifelong wards.

How well the Geel approach, now under the direction of the State Psychiatric Hospital, has worked can be seen from the experience of two patients who were photographed in 1961. One of them *(left)* is a young man whom the hospital nicknamed Jan, to protect his identity. The other is an old woman called Marieke by the hospital. Except for Geel both probably would have wound up in institutions leading empty lives. But the Geel approach placed them with families and made them feel wanted; years later both were leading happy and productive lives in Geel.

A secure niche in a foster family

For 16-year-old Jan, absorption into a Geel family provided a uniquely effective chance to gain self-confidence and to learn to function in the everyday world. In a hospital he probably would have been isolated with similarly handicapped patients of his own age, subjected to institutional routine and discipline, and excluded from the normal world. But in Geel he could enjoy the attention and affection of his adopted family, go to school just like anybody else, develop useful skills, and mingle freely with people of every age and description in a healthy environment.

Working with his foster father, Jan helps repair a motorcycle belonging to the family. Gradually, he took on more and more responsibilities, until he could handle a job in the family flour mill, running errands and helping the truck drivers make their deliveries.

Jan grins in enjoyment at his turn in an animated game of cards. "We sat down and played cards a lot," one family member recalled. It was a custom that brought all of Jan's foster relatives together for joint activity and heightened the boy's feelings of belonging.

"I want you to be nicely dressed before you go off to school," Jan's foster mother tells him after buttoning his shirt and tucking in his collar. Young patients are taught the same standards of personal hygiene, grooming and behavior as other children in their foster families.

Although placed in a class with younger children, Jan is treated like any other pupil by a teacher explaining a math problem. Regular classroom attendance was judged appropriate for Jan, but Geel usually provides only occupational therapy or vocational training for young patients. Most of the children who require classroom education are given special instruction elsewhere.

Jan gestures to make a point in an
animated conversation with a friendly
passerby. Frequent, informal contacts with
friends and strangers in Geel enabled
him to develop a confident, easy manner.

Like any healthy European youngster,
Jan takes his turn kicking a soccer ball.
Such activities were essential to his
progress, helping him develop the motor
skills and coordination that are part of
normal adolescent growth but that often
are neglected among the mentally ill.

A useful and warm old age

The majority of the patients in Geel are chronically ill adults—many of them in their twilight years, like Marieke, the old woman at left. If they are confined to conventional mental institutions, such elderly patients usually languish in loneliness, awaiting a graceless death as their mental and physical capacities rapidly decline in an environment that makes no demands on them.

The Geel system offers a humane alternative for such people as Marieke. Busy at work in a rustic kitchen, she led an active and useful life, helping to care for her surrogate family.

With a toddler at her side and another of her adopted family's children watching her affectionately, the aging mental patient called Marieke prepares lunch in an old-fashioned, homey kitchen.

*The children's grandmother (center)
looks on approvingly while they play a
game with Marieke. Although an adopted
member of the family, Marieke is
accepted as a sort of second grandmother.*

Marieke's surrogate grandchildren enjoy helping with one of her daily chores—feeding the chickens.

Held by her mother, the youngest member of the family affectionately pats Marieke on the cheek.

A trusted family member, Marieke goes
on a shopping expedition to a nearby
grocery store, where (above) a clerk is
ready to help as she pays for provisions
she has selected. Storekeepers and
their fellow townsmen in Geel, long
accustomed to family-care patients, treat
them with courtesy and friendliness,
quietly coming to their assistance only
when necessary. As a result, Marieke and
others have found in Geel a community
and family that appreciate their efforts
while understanding their limitations.

Bibliography

Aldrin, Edwin E., and Wayne Warga, *Return to Earth*. Random House, Inc., 1973.

Alexander, Franz G., and Sheldon T. Selesnick, *The History of Psychiatry*. Harper & Row, Publishers, 1966.

Arieti, Silvano, ed., *American Handbook of Psychiatry*, Vols. I-III. Basic Books, Inc., 1974.

Beck, Aaron T., *Depression*. University of Pennsylvania Press, 1970.

Bergin, Allen E., and Sol L. Garfield, eds., *Handbook of Psychotherapy and Behavior Change*. John Wiley & Sons, Inc., 1971.

Bettelheim, Bruno:
The Empty Fortress. The Free Press, 1967.
A Home for the Heart. Alfred A. Knopf, Inc., 1972.

Brenner, Charles, *An Elementary Textbook of Psychoanalysis*. Anchor Books, 1974.

Brill, A. A., ed., *The Basic Writings of Sigmund Freud*. Modern Library, Inc., 1965.

Bry, Adelaide, ed., *Inside Psychotherapy*. Basic Books, Inc., 1972.

Calder, Nigel, *The Mind of Man*. Viking Press, Inc., 1971.

Coleman, James C., *Abnormal Psychology and Modern Life*. Scott, Foresman & Company, 1956.

Davison, Gerald C., and John M. Neale, *Abnormal Psychology: An Experimental Clinical Approach*. John Wiley & Sons, Inc., 1974.

Eaton, Joseph W., and Robert J. Weil, *Culture and Mental Disorders*. The Free Press, 1955.

Flach, Frederic F., *The Secret Strength of Depression*. J. B. Lippincott Company, 1974.

Flach, Frederic F., and Suzanne C. Draghi, *The Nature and Treatment of Depression*. John Wiley & Sons, Inc., 1975.

Freud, Sigmund, *Collected Papers*, Vol. 3, James Strachey, ed. Basic Books, Inc., 1959.

Grant, Vernon W., *Great Abnormals*. Hawthorn Books, Inc., 1968.

Greenwald, Harold, ed., *Great Cases in Psychoanalysis*. Ballantine Books, Inc., 1974.

Haggard, Howard W., *Devils, Drugs, and Doctors*. Harper & Row, Publishers, 1929.

Hendin, Herbert, *Suicide and Scandinavia*. Grune & Stratton, Inc., 1964.

Herman, Melvin, and Lucy Freeman, *The Pursuit of Mental Health*. Macmillan Publishing Co., Inc., 1974.

Hirai, Tomio, Sr., *Psychophysiology of Zen*. Igaku Shoin Ltd., 1974.

Horney, Karen, *The Neurotic Personality of Our Time*. W. W. Norton & Company, Inc., 1964.

Kaplan, Bert, ed., *The Inner World of Mental Illness*. Harper & Row, Publishers, 1964.

Kiev, Ari, *Transcultural Psychiatry*. Penguin Books, Inc., 1972.

Kleinmuntz, Benjamin, *Essentials of Abnormal Psychology*. Harper & Row, Publishers, 1974.

Kline, Nathan S., *From Sad to Glad*. G. P. Putnam's Sons, 1974.

Kubie, Lawrence S., *Practical and Theoretical Aspects of Psychoanalysis*. International Universities Press, Inc., 1957.

Laing, R. D., *The Divided Self*. Penguin Books Ltd., 1973.

Langner, Thomas S., and Stanley T. Michael, *Life Stress and Mental Health*. The Free Press, 1963.

London, Perry, *The Modes and Morals of Psychotherapy*. Holt, Rinehart & Winston, Inc., 1964.

London, Perry, and David Rosenhan, eds., *Foundations of Abnormal Psychology*. Holt, Rinehart & Winston, Inc., 1968.

Maher, Brendan A., ed.:
Contemporary Abnormal Psychology. Penguin Books, Inc., 1973.
Progress in Experimental Personality Research, Vols. I and V. Academic Press, Inc., 1970.

May, Rollo, ed., *Existential Psychology*. Random House, Inc., 1961.

May, Rollo, Ernest Angel and Henri Ellenberger, eds., *Existence: A New Dimension in Psychiatry and Psychology*. Simon & Schuster, Inc., 1958.

Medvedev, Zhores A., and Roy A., *A Question of Madness*. Alfred A. Knopf, Inc., 1971.

Mendels, Joseph, *Concepts of Depression*. John Wiley & Sons, Inc., 1970.

Menninger, Karl:
Theory of Psychoanalytic Technique. Harper & Row, Publishers, 1964.
The Vital Balance. Viking Press, Inc., 1974.

Murphy, Jane M., and Alexander H. Leighton, eds., *Approaches to Cross-Cultural Psychiatry*. Cornell University Press, 1966.

Nathan, Peter E., and Sandra L. Harris, *Psychopathology and Society*. McGraw-Hill Book Company, 1975.

Nijinsky, Romola, *Nijinsky*. Simon & Schuster, Inc., 1934.

Oates, Wayne, *Confessions of a Workaholic*. World Publishing Co., 1971.

Oliver, Paul, *The Story of the Blues*. Chilton Book Company, 1969.

Ostow, Mortimer, *The Psychology of Melancholy*. Harper & Row, Publishers, 1970.

Ray, Marie Beynon, *Doctors of the Mind*. Charter Books, 1963.

Rexford, Eveoleen N., ed., *Journal of Child Psychiatry*. Quadrangle Books, 1971.

Rimland, Bernard, *Infantile Autism*. Appleton-Century-Crofts, 1964.

Schofield, William, *Psychotherapy: The Purchase of Friendship*. Prentice-Hall, Inc., 1964.

Sitwell, Edith, *English Eccentrics*. Vanguard Press, Inc., 1957.

Snyder, Solomon H., *Madness and the Brain*. McGraw-Hill Book Company, 1974.

Srole, Leo, et al., *Mental Health in the Metropolis*. McGraw-Hill Book Company, 1962.

Szasz, Thomas S., *The Age of Madness*. Anchor Books, 1973.

Taylor, Norman, *Plant Drugs that Changed the World*. Dodd, Mead & Co., 1965.

Thigpen, Corbett H., and Hervey M. Cleckley, *The Three Faces of Eve*. McGraw-Hill Book Company, 1957.

Tomsen, Robert, *Bill W*. Harper & Row, Publishers, 1975.

Zilboorg, Gregory, and George W. Henry, *A History of Medical Psychology*. W. W. Norton & Company, Inc., 1941.

Picture Credits

The sources for the illustrations in this book are shown below. Credits from left to right are separated by semicolons, from top to bottom by dashes.

Cover—Jay Maisel. 6—Gene Laurents. 11 —Picture Collection, Branch Libraries, The New York Public Library. 13 through 16—© Tony Ray Jones from Magnum. 20,21—Courtesy Alcoholics Anonymous World Services. 25—Gerald Martineau, *The Washington Post.* 27—© copyright 1966 United Features Syndicate, Inc. 29 —Charles Gatewood. 32 through 45— Charles Harbutt from Magnum. 46— Dan Budnik. 51—Culver Pictures. 54,55 —© Jill Krementz—Inge Morath from Magnum; Elliott Erwitt from Magnum. 58—Edmund Engelman. 61—Don Hogan Charles for *The New York Times.* 64—Michael Weisbrot. 69,70—Quentin Bell. 71 —Quentin Bell (2)—Camera Press Ltd.; From *Downhill All the Way,* copyright © 1967 by Leonard Woolf, reproduced by permission of Mrs. Ian Parsons and Harcourt Brace Jovanovich, Inc. 72—Gisèle Freund. 75—John Hearst Jr. for the *New York Daily Mirror.* Overlapping chart based on statistics provided by the World Health Organization. 78—Record labels courtesy Ben M. Hall. Words and music of "Blues Before Sunrise" by Leroy Carr, © copyright 1950, 1963 by MCA Music, a Division of MCA Inc., New York, N.Y. Used by permission/All rights reserved. 80,81—Edward Clark from TIME-LIFE Picture Agency. 84—Eivind Vorland. 87 —T. Tanuma from TIME-LIFE Picture Agency. 88 through 99—Gilles Peress from Magnum. 100—TIME-LIFE Picture Agency. 103—The Mansell Collection. 106,107—Richard Walker. 109—Reprinted with permission of Macmillan Publishing Co., Inc., from *Mental Institutions in America* by Gerald N. Grob, copyright © 1973 by The Free Press, a Division of Macmillan Publishing Co., Inc. 110—Ken Heyman. 115—Herb Goro. 116,117—Barry Kaufman from his book *Son-Rise,* published by Harper & Row Publishers Inc. 118—Barry Kaufman. 122 through 133—Bill Eppridge. 134—Chester Higgins. 137—Walter Bennett from TIME-LIFE Picture Agency. 139—Chart based on statistics provided by the U.S. Public Health Service. 140,141—Ken Kay. 144 —Michael Hardy courtesy The Arbours Association, 55 Dartmouth Park Road, London, N.W. 5. 147 through 150— Charles Biasiny. 153—Adapted from chart prepared by Robert W. Earle, California College of Medicine, U.C. at Irvine. 155—Ben Ross. 158 through 171 —James H. Karales.

Acknowledgments

The author and editors of this book wish to thank the following persons and institutions: Ignacio Aguilar, Director, Xipe-Totec Mental Health Clinic, Metropolitan State Hospital, Norwalk, California; Dr. Roger Ballard, Department of Psychology, University of Leeds, England; Quentin Bell, Beddingham, Sussex, England; Dr. Jeanluc Bernot, President, Committee for Research on Alcoholism, Paris; Giorgio Bignami, Research Assistant, Laboratory of Therapeutic Chemistry, Instituto Superiore Di Sanita, Rome; Dr. Gerhard Bosch, Director, Rheinische Landesklinik für Jugend und Kinderpsychiatrie, Süchteln, West Germany; G. W. Brown, Professor of Sociology, Bedford College, London; Dr. T. J. Crow, Clinical Research Centre, Northwick Park Hospital, London; Eberhard de Haan, Federal Organization for Workers' Welfare, Bonn; Dominique Diatkine, Paris; Dr. Gilbert Diatkine, Paris; Marie-France Dréau, Press Attaché, Société Française de Production, Paris; Dr. Edward Eismann, Assistant Professor of Psychiatry, Albert Einstein College of Medicine, Yeshiva University, New York; Dr. Ian Falloon, Psychological Treatment Section, Maudsley Hospital, London; Jean-Pierre Ferrant, Director of Centre de la Membrolle, Tours-sur-Choisille, France; Professor Franco Giberti, Director, Psychiatric Clinic, University of Genoa, Italy; Professor D. G. Grahame-Smith, Medical Research Council's Clinical Pharmacology Unit, Radcliffe Infirmary, Oxford, England; Dr. I. L. Iversen, MRC Neurochemical Pharmacology Unit, Cambridge, England; Dr. Rana Kartal, Head Psychiatrist, Evangelisches Krankenhaus, Gelsenkirchen, West Germany; Dr. Ari Kiev, Director of Social Psychiatry, Research Institute, New York City; Ed Long, Deputy Director, Division of Scientific and Public Information, National Institute of Mental Health, Rockville, Maryland; Angelo Lusso, Center for Mental Hygiene, Turin, Italy; Dr. B. M. Mandelbrote, Littlemore Hospital, Oxford, England; Dr. H. Matheussen, Medical Director, The State Psychiatric Hospital Center for Family Care, Geel, Belgium; Luciano Mecacci, Assistant, C.N.R. Institute of Psychology, Rome; Ivor Mills, Professor of Medicine, Cambridge University, England; Lucia Monami, Institute of Psychology, Pontifica Universita Salesiana, Rome; Jean-François Moreaux, Press Attaché, INSEE, Paris; Lynn Okerson, therapist and assistant to Dr. Ari Kiev, New York City; Dr. Morris Parloff, National Institute of Mental Health, Rockville, Maryland; Michele Piccione, Assistant, Clinic for Nervous and Mental Diseases, Rome University, Italy; Dr. John Richer, Research Psychologist, Smith Hospital, Henley-on-Thames, England; Professor Pietro Sarteschi, Director, Center for the Prevention and Therapy of Depression, Psychiatric Clinic, Pisa University, Italy; Dr. Jan Schrijvers, Medical Director for Family Nursing, The State Psychiatric Hospital Center for Family Care, Geel, Belgium; Dr. Gernot Sonneck, Center for Crisis Intervention, Vienna; Dr. Leo Srole, Professor of Social Sciences, Department of Psychiatry, Columbia University, New York City; R. Williams, Department of Prints and Drawings, British Museum, London; Dr. G. Terence Wilson, Assistant Professor of Psychology, Graduate School of Applied and Professional Psychology, Rutgers University, New Brunswick, New Jersey; Dr. Virginia N. Wood, Consultant, Xipe-Totec Mental Health Clinic, Metropolitan State Hospital, Norwalk, California.

Index

Numerals in italics indicate a photograph or drawing of the subject mentioned.

Printed in U.S.A.

Connections!

MONEY

CAROLINE GRIMSHAW

TEXT EDITOR

IQBAL HUSSAIN

CONSULTANT

DR JANE COLLIER

JUDGE INSTITUTE OF MANAGEMENT STUDIES, UNIVERSITY OF CAMBRIDGE

ILLUSTRATIONS

NICK DUFFY ☆ SPIKE GERRELL ☆ JO MOORE

World Book

in association with

W C N

connections!

MONEY

CREATIVE AND EDITORIAL DIRECTOR
CONCEPT/FORMAT/DESIGN/TEXT
CAROLINE GRIMSHAW

TEXT EDITOR
IQBAL HUSSAIN

CONSULTANT
DR JANE COLLIER

JUDGE INSTITUTE OF MANAGEMENT STUDIES, UNIVERSITY OF CAMBRIDGE

ILLUSTRATIONS
**NICK DUFFY ☆ SPIKE GERRELL
JO MOORE**

THANKS TO
LAURA CARTWRIGHT PICTURE RESEARCH
BRONWEN LEWIS EDITORIAL SUPPORT
AND **ANDREW JARVIS ☆ TIM SANPHER
CHARLES SHAAR MURRAY**

**TITLES
IN THIS
SERIES** →
☆ ART
☆ BUILDINGS
☆ EARTH
☆ MACHINES
☆ MONEY
☆ MUSIC
☆ PEOPLE

FIRST PUBLISHED IN THE UNITED STATES AND CANADA BY
WORLD BOOK, INC.
525 W. MONROE
CHICAGO, IL 60661
IN ASSOCIATION WITH TWO-CAN PUBLISHING LTD.

COPYRIGHT © CAROLINE GRIMSHAW 1997.
ALL RIGHTS RESERVED. NO PART OF THIS PUBLICATION MAY BE REPRODUCED, STORED IN A
RETRIEVAL SYSTEM OR TRANSMITTED IN ANY FORM OR BY ANY MEANS ELECTRONIC,
MECHANICAL, PHOTOCOPYING, RECORDING OR OTHERWISE, WITHOUT WRITTEN PERMISSION
FROM THE PUBLISHER.

FOR INFORMATION ON OTHER WORLD BOOK PRODUCTS,
CALL 1-800-255-1750, X 2238, OR VISIT US AT OUR WEB SITE AT
HTTP://WWW.WORLDBOOK.COM

GRIMSHAW, CAROLINE.
   MONEY/CAROLINE GRIMSHAW: TEXT EDITOR IQBAL HUSSAIN :
ILLUSTRATIONS NICK DUFFY, SPIKE GERRELL, JO MOORE.
   P. CM. — (CONNECTIONS!)
   SUMMARY: BRIEF TEXT, ILLUSTRATIONS, QUIZZES, AND ACTIVIITIES INTRODUCE THE
HISTORY, USES, AND EFFECTS OF MONEY.
   INCLUDES INDEX.
   ISBN 0-7166-1308-5 (HC). — ISBN 0-7166-1309-3 (SC)
   1. MONEY—JUVENILE LITERATURE. [1. MONEY—MISCELLANEA. 2. QUESTIONS AND
ANSWERS.] I. HUSSAIN, IQBAL. II. DUFFY, NICK, ILL. III. GERRELL, SPIKE, ILL. IV. MOORE, JO,
ILL. V. TITLE. VI. SERIES: CONNECTIONS! (CHICAGO, ILL.)
HG221.5.G735 1998
332.4—DC21   97-17275

PRINTED IN HONG KONG
1 2 3 4 5 6 7 8 9 10 01 00 99 98 97

Contents

**DISCOVER THE CONNECTIONS THROUGH
QUESTIONS AND ANSWERS...**
YOU CAN READ THIS BOOK FROM START TO FINISH OR
LEAPFROG THROUGH THE SECTIONS
FOLLOWING THE PATHS SUGGESTED
IN THESE SPECIAL "CONNECT! BOXES."

Connect!

**ENJOY YOUR JOURNEY OF
DISCOVERY AND UNDERSTANDING**